Gifts and Ministries
of the
Holy Spirit

Gifts and Ministries
of the
Holy Spirit

by
Dr. Lester Sumrall

HARRISON HOUSE
Tulsa, Oklahoma

Unless otherwise indicated,
all Scripture quotations are taken from
the *King James Version* of the Bible.

2nd Printing
Over 17,000 in Print

Gifts and Ministries of the Holy Spirit
ISBN 0-89274-189-9
Copyright © 1982 by Lester Sumrall
P. O. Box 12
South Bend, Indiana 46624

Published by Harrison House, Inc.
P. O. Box 35035
Tulsa, Oklahoma 74135

Dedication

This study on the gifts and ministries of the Holy Spirit is dedicated to the late Howard Carter of London, England.

While Rev. Carter was serving time in prison as a conscientious objector during World War I, he spent many hours in prayer and study of the Word of God. It was there that these glorious truths regarding the gifts of the Spirit were revealed to him.

I lived with Howard Carter for a number of years and knew personally how he was persecuted by religious leaders because of these truths. Yet today his explanation of the gifts of the Spirit are accepted and enjoyed by millions of people of all denominations throughout the world.

Many times I was highly honored to hear him lecture and answer questions on the gifts of the Spirit. The entire charismatic world today owes the treasure of this teaching to this dedicated man to whom God revealed the identity, definition, and operation of the gifts of the Holy Spirit.

I certainly do thank God for my having known Howard Carter, for the privilege of living with him, and for the truths that I am permitted to share with you because of this friend of years past.

Contents

Preface

As we begin this study into the gifts and ministries of the Holy Spirit, I cannot emphasize strongly enough the need for information on this subject. As I so often say when teaching, God cannot bless ignorance; He can only bless intelligence.

Do you wish to have faith? I am quite sure that you do. Then you must realize this fact: You can have faith only in relation to your knowledge of God. The same principle stands true with regard to the gifts and ministries of the Holy Spirit. These gifts and ministries function with greatest accuracy through people who understand them.

The purpose in this study is to define the gifts and ministries of the Holy Spirit and to reveal their operations in the Body of Christ today.

If God's Holy Spirit is to function fully in our lives, we must have an open heart and a consuming desire to know all we can about the nature and role of the Holy Spirit — His gifts and His ministries to the Body of Christ. It is my earnest prayer that this book be a helpful tool in fulfilling your need.

Part I
Gifts of the
Holy Spirit

Now concerning spiritual gifts, brethren, I would not have you ignorant. Ye know that ye were Gentiles, carried away unto these dumb idols, even as ye were led.

Wherefore I give you to understand, that no man speaking by the Spirit of God calleth Jesus accursed: and that no man can say that Jesus is the Lord, but by the Holy Ghost.

Now there are diversities of gifts, but the same Spirit. And there are differences of administrations, but the same Lord. And there are diversities of operations, but it is the same God which worketh all in all. But the manifestation of the Spirit is given to every man (and woman) to profit withal.

For to one is given by the Spirit the word of wisdom; to another the word of knowledge by the same Spirit; to another faith by the same Spirit; to another the gifts of healing by the same Spirit; to another the working of miracles; to another prophecy; to another discerning of spirits; to another divers kinds of tongues; to another the interpretation of tongues.

But all these worketh that one and the selfsame Spirit, dividing to every man severally as he will.

1 Corinthians 12:1-11

Introduction

There is no other subject so pertinent to the world scene today as the operation of spiritual gifts in the Body of Christ. The gifts of the Spirit — the weapons of our warfare — can destroy any force the Devil might use against the Body of Christ.

I want you to realize how tremendous the gifts of the Spirit can be as they function in *your* life. You are a candidate for these gifts — not for one gift only, but for all nine of them.

A number of years ago in a simple wooden building in Tennessee, God showed me a vision. (I have experienced only two in my entire life.) In this vision I saw millions of people marching past me into eternity. At that time God made me to know that I was called to minister to the entire world.

At that same time in London, England, a man I had never heard of — Rev. Howard Carter — also received a special message from God, saying he would travel and minister throughout the world. Howard Carter was then president of Hampstead Bible College in North London. At that time God also told him: "I have a companion for you. He shall come from afar. He will be a stranger when he comes, and these are the words he will say . . ." This message from God so impressed Rev. Carter that he recorded word for word what God had said to him.

At the time Howard Carter came to minister in this country, I was preaching an open-air revival for a church in the state of Oklahoma. One morning as I was kneeling in prayer under a tree, the Lord spoke these words to my heart: "Close this meeting today

13

and go to Eureka Springs." Eureka Springs is a town in Arkansas about two hundred miles away.

Immediately, I went to the sponsoring pastor's house and told him my plans. This man, much older than I and very severe, scolded me for wanting to close the meeting and said he would never recommend me to other pastors.

So, leaving the angry pastor behind, I headed for Eureka Springs.

In Eureka Springs, I found the great camp-meeting in which an Englishman, who turned out to be Howard Carter, was speaking. The meeting hall was packed with people. When Rev. Carter finished ministering, he walked out to the sidewalk and began greeting the people. When he reached me, words began to flow out of my mouth. They were the same words God had spoken to him in London almost eighteen months before.

"Brother Carter," I said, "I will do what you do and I will go where you go. If you travel by plane, I will do likewise. If you go by train, so will I. If you walk, I will walk." With these words God fulfilled to the letter the message He had given Rev. Carter in London.

Because I didn't realize what was happening, I became upset with myself for saying foolish things to a stranger. But Rev. Carter sensed something very different, so he took hold of my hand. When he did, I said, "When you are old, I will help you. I will strengthen you and bless you."

And this I did, until the time he went to be with God in heaven.

Rev. Carter invited me to his hotel room and read from his book of prophecies. He read the words that God had revealed to him that I would say. Through this amazing experience, I realized that the Word of Wisdom is true, that God can show us the future. There in Eureka Springs we lifted our hearts and thanked God that He would speak to us in these last days. In that moment there began a most remarkable friendship. Howard Carter and I traveled throughout the world ministering together — he as a teacher, I as an evangelist — and blessing multitudes of people.

The Night Vision

Here you can see the functioning of the Word of God's Wisdom. God did not reveal everything to me. All He did at first was show me a dying world. That night I made my commitment and began to get myself ready to minister to the whole world. Then He took me one step at a time.

I was so excited that day that I left without asking Howard Carter where he was going, and I forgot to give him my address. Within one hour, I had lost him! It was through the gifts of the Spirit that I found him again.

My sister was traveling with me in evangelistic work at the time, so I drove her to our parents' home. While there, I intended to sell my car and find Howard Carter — wherever he might be in the world. With the Depression on, selling a car was not an easy task. And getting a passport in those days was quite an experience. The only place I could get one was Washington, D.C., and they issued them just as quickly or slowly as they wanted.

It was three months before I could get everything done, and by that time I had no idea where Mr. Carter was. Some people said he had gone to China, others said Japan, still others said India. Finally, I asked the Lord, "Lord, where is this man?" His answer was interesting. All He said was: "Go to the bottom and work up." (God often leads us like that. If He told us the whole story, we would know too much.)

So I started at "the bottom." I found a British boat headed for Australia and got on board. Twenty-one days later the boat docked in Wellington, New Zealand. When I stepped off the boat, I had no idea where Howard Carter was; but, determined to find him for fellowship, I began looking for a Full Gospel church. To my amazement, Howard Carter was in New Zealand!

Mr. Carter was attending a minister's retreat in the mountains where there was no communication of any kind. While Mr. Carter was in prayer, God moved again by the gifts of the Spirit. He later told me the following story:

It seems that a day earlier, Mr. Carter was praying, "Lord, over three months ago you gave me a young man, but I have lost him."

The Lord said, "No, you haven't."

"But, Lord, I haven't heard from him since."

The Lord said, "He is in Wellington harbor right now on a boat. Tomorrow morning he will leave that boat, looking for a church, so send the pastor down with a note to him. Tell him you will meet him in Australia."

Mr. Carter walked out where the pastors were and asked, "Which one of you is from the city of Wellington?"

When a man raised his hand, Mr. Carter said to him, "Tomorrow morning there will be a young man at your house. His name is Lester Sumrall. He will be asking for me. Tell him I'll meet him in Australia. Will you give him my personal card?"

The next morning, I started looking around town. After two or three hours I arrived at a little white chapel on the hill. When the pastor answered the door, I said, "I am Lester Sumrall. I am from America. You don't know me."

He said, "Yes, I do. Howard Carter told me you would be here. Here is a note from him to you."

Together we saw the working of the gifts of the Spirit in a most wonderful way in our lives. Rev. Carter had these gifts functioning almost constantly in his ministry, never foolishly, but for great things. God put us together as a team, and we went around the world as teacher and evangelist, winning many souls to Jesus, setting up Bible schools, doing all the things God wanted us to do.

Through my relationship with Howard Carter I gained a firsthand knowledge of the operation of the Holy Spirit. I heard him teach on this subject, not just once or twice, but many times. In Indonesia, Australia, China, Japan, Poland, England, South America, the United States, I heard this man share with people about the gifts of the Spirit. I never wearied of it. Each time he would lecture, I was engrossed. Because of that experience, I am able to bring you knowledge that others may not be fortunate enough to have.

When Howard Carter laid hands on me, he said, "The spiritual life and the faith that is within my heart, I put into you." I trembled throughout my total being as that man of God, twice my age, laid his hands on me to transmit to me the faith that was in his own heart.

I believe God ordained that segment of my past so I could share with the Body of Christ today in a direct line from the one who in these modern times found these gifts by the power of the Holy Ghost. God planted them within him. Before Howard Carter's time, people misunderstood and minimized the gifts of the Spirit. They said the gift of faith meant just to believe for something. If you had the gift of the word of wisdom, they assumed that meant you were just clever or smart. Howard Carter recognized these as *sign gifts* from God, and he defined them. Today multiplied millions of people have accepted the truth as it was revealed to his heart.

I believe God wants to accomplish His work supernaturally on the face of the earth. He wants to take natural people and work supernaturally through them to bring about a mighty surge of His power, just the way He worked through Howard Carter. I challenge you to make yourself ready for Him to use you in this wonderful moment in which we live today.

1
Nature and Role of the Holy Spirit

To accurately study the work of the Holy Spirit, we must begin with the Book of Genesis, the first book of the Bible. First Corinthians 12:1-11 includes the first mention in the New Testament of the *works* of the Holy Spirit, which are the *gifts* of the Spirit; but in the Book of Genesis we see the Holy Spirit introduced in pristine grandeur — an exciting and thrilling display of the Holy Spirit as He functions best.

In the very first verses of the Bible, we read:

In the beginning God created the heaven and the earth. And the earth was without form, and void; and darkness was upon the face of the deep.

And the Spirit of God moved upon the face of the waters.

And God said, Let there be light: and there was light (Gen. 1:1-3).

The functioning of the Holy Spirit as demonstrated in the early Christian Church is not new. He had been working with human beings for 4,000 years prior to the Christian era, and He has been working in the Church for the 2,000 years since. The Holy Spirit has been very busy functioning in behalf of mankind for 6,000 years. He knows our problems; He knows the answers; and we need these answers from Him.

Omnipotence of the Spirit

When we think of the functioning of the Holy Spirit in the creation of the world, we think of omnipotence. The Holy Spirit was omnipotent, all-powerful. Out of the chaos that existed in the beginning, He brought cosmos. God spoke, and His Word had to be obeyed! The Spirit of God moved upon the desolation, and there came forth that which was beautiful for God and for man.

Omnipresence of the Spirit

In His creative powers the Holy Spirit is omnipotent. In His universality He is omnipresent. Psalm 139:7 says this: *Whither shall I go from thy spirit? or whither shall I flee from thy presence?* Here David is saying to God, "Where could I go to escape the presence of Your Spirit?" It is impossible to flee from the presence of the Holy Spirit. Perhaps you found that to be true when you were running away from your convictions. God "dogged" you until He got you — and He can do it again and again!

The Holy Spirit is universal in the fulfilling of His operations. He possesses all power and He is everywhere. There is no place that the gifts of the Spirit will not work. They will function anywhere, whether it be in Asia, South America, Europe, or right where you are now.

In Genesis 6:3, we find how God said in words of convicting strength and power that His Spirit would not always strive with man. The Holy Spirit strives to bring man into a place of reconciliation with God. Imagine that happening from Genesis and continuing through Revelation. The Holy Spirit has a fullness of ministry whose chief exercise is to cause men to come to God. Jesus, in speaking to us of the functionings of the Holy Spirit, told us that the Holy Spirit would be a comfort to us and that He would relate the things He heard in the heavens. He would relate those things you say to God and then tell you what God says in reply.

It is the Holy Spirit Who moves back and forth, bringing communication from our hearts to God and from God's heart to us. He is accustomed to striving with men's hearts. When you feel within you a craving and a desire to be more like God and to live a holy life, that is the moving and the functioning of the Holy Spirit in your behalf.

Poured Out upon All Flesh

During this present age, the Dispensation of Grace, God is pouring out of His Spirit upon all flesh. *And it shall come to pass in the last days, saith God, I will pour out of my Spirit upon all flesh* (Acts 2:17). Here is the central theme of this study: The Spirit of God will be poured out upon us. We shall experience the infilling of the Spirit of God; and as the infilling of the Spirit of God comes, these gifts will automatically flow.

I will tell you how these gifts came to start functioning in my life. You may be interested to know that they were born, not in a moment of jubilation or victory in my life, but in a moment of great attrition. They were born in a moment when I was downcast and almost broken, which only made me realize the greatness and majesty of God. I came to know the thrill of having God in my own heart and life. I believe it will be exciting to you, too, as the power of the Holy Ghost comes upon you and the gifts of the Spirit begin to function in your life.

If the gifts of the Spirit were not for you, it would be wrong for me to discuss them in this way. If

21

they were only for the hierarchy of the Church — for the bishops and the archbishops — then you and I might as well discuss something else. We would need to study a subject that is available to us, something we can use in our everyday lives, something that can help with our everyday burdens and trials and cares. God wants it to work, and it *will* work. It *does* work.

In the last days I will pour out of my Spirit upon all flesh. "All flesh" means men, women, young people — all cultures, all languages, all people — whether lowborn or highborn, well-educated or ignorant.

The fact that God is willing at this time to pour out His Spirit upon all flesh makes this study imperative. We are at a moment when, more than ever before in the history of man, the power of the Holy Spirit is being poured out. I don't want to be left in a dry corner; I want to be standing right in the middle of the deluge! I want the blessing of God in its fullest. I want to be in the middle of the spout where the glory comes out!

Speaking of the Holy Ghost, Jesus said, *Howbeit when he, the Spirit of truth, is come, he will guide you into all truth: for he shall not speak of himself; but whatsoever he shall hear, that shall he speak: and he will shew you things to come* (John 16:13).

One of the functions of the Holy Spirit is to bring to our hearts a revelation of the future. If we need to know things that are to come to pass, and the ways in which they shall come to pass, the Holy Spirit is the One to reveal them. We need not go to a fortune-teller or to an astrologer. We can go directly to the Holy Ghost. We have a prophecy from our Lord and

Savior that the Holy Spirit will be the One to show us things to come.

The Holy Spirit is our guide into all truth, the revealer of things to come. The Holy Spirit is living in His own dispensation today — separate from the Dispensation of Innocence, the Dispensation of Conscience, the Dispensation of Human Government, the Dispensation of Promise, the Dispensation of the Law. We are now living in the Dispensation of the Grace of the Holy Ghost; and while living in His own dispensation with Him, we can expect His movements to be greater than ever before.

Able Ministers

In 1 Peter 4:10, we read these beautiful words: *As every man hath received the gift, even so minister the same one to another . . . .* To me this is one of the most precious verses of Scripture that has been delivered to us from the Word of God. They that have received the gifts should minister the same.

I believe that anything which has been given to us was given to us of God to share. God does not dig holes and bury things. He is not a cover-up man; that is the Devil's business. God is a *revealer*, a revealer of the interior workings of human beings. This great message of the gifts of the Holy Spirit is something that should be shared. That is the purpose of this writing.

I encourage you to become a sharer and to share everything you receive. In fact, the way to get this message to grow in your own spirit is to start talking to others about the things you have learned. As you talk about them, there will almost immediately be an increase of knowledge on your

23

own part. As you give, you receive. The Bible says that they that water are watered. As you give out, you will receive back. That is especially true as we study the Word of God. They that have received the gift should minister the same. This is the desire of my own heart.

I have shared these preliminary thoughts relating to the Spirit of God for a specific reason: The deeper I can place the foundations of this truth, the stronger your tower of strength will be, and I want it to be very strong!

In 2 Corinthians 3:6, the Word of God says we should be able ministers, giving life. I would say that the deep purpose of these lessons would be for us to become able ministers of truth, giving life — spiritual life, dynamic life — to those with whom we come in contact.

2
Charismatic Renewal

Possibly the most spiritual revolution since the Protestant Reformation is taking place in the world at this moment. This is a tremendous statement, but one which I believe to be true. A new force has appeared within Christian ranks today. Nothing has so stirred and excited the entire Christian world during our generation as the movement referred to as the "charismatic renewal."

Unlimited by authority and unconcerned about the organized church, this ecumenical following, which is composed of many colorful backgrounds, is marching toward an experience that is completely in line and in total harmony with New Testament truth.

The "charismatic renewal" is said to be the fastest growing religious movement since New Testament days, having grown quickly and in many directions. People from every Christian denominational background are coming together, equally eager to receive truth on the charismatic gifts of the Holy Spirit.

During the first half of the twentieth century, the most despised segment of the Christian Church was known as "pentecostalism." Suddenly these pentecostals have become the most important spiritual factor on the face of the earth.

In the decade of the 1960s multitudes within the so-called traditional churches — Catholics, Episcopalians, Lutherans, Methodists, Baptists, and others — started receiving the infilling of the Holy Spirit, just as was experienced by the early disciples on the day of Pentecost, evidenced by a phenomenon called "speaking in other tongues."

"Tongues" is a spiritual language coming from the spiritual person — not from the "soulical" parts (the mind), but from the spirit. The words spoken cannot be understood by the mind. In this experience God gives the speaker what is termed a "heavenly language," or a "prayer language."

It was a remarkable and amazing event to the protestant world when Catholics began to move in spiritual realities, bypassing the entire fundamental and orthodox denominations, entering into the ranks of the pentecostals — those who believed the whole Bible to be the Full Gospel. When the Spirit began to move them into the salvation rank of regeneration, they went on into the fullness of the baptism of the Holy Spirit. To me it is remarkable that they did not stop halfway. They did not stop on second base, but ran on around. If they were going to have anything, they would have it all — and they received, much to the amazement of millions of people!

Multitudes of people in this charismatic renewal meet in colleges, in private homes, in borrowed halls. They meet in the most unlikely and unusual places to worship their God and His beloved Son, the Lord Jesus Christ. The gifts of the Spirit function wherever they meet — whether it is in a church, a home, an office building, an auditorium, or a convention hall.

This clearly demonstrates that God has no holy places. He will meet you anywhere — the home, the factory, the street — wherever you are.

Charisma Today

Many people teach that after the day of Pentecost, the phenomena of "charisma" ceased. For people to say that God cannot do today what He was doing 2,000 years ago shows me they do not know the God I know. My God can do anything today that He did then. We are not eating the leftovers of a feast; we are taking in the whole menu. We are getting in on the best and the biggest that the world has ever known.

Proof of this is in Acts, chapter 2. On the day of Pentecost Peter stood and spontaneously began to preach. Under the anointing of the Holy Spirit, he laid open the Word of God and preached with such strength and power that the people trembled at his words. When he had finished speaking, verse 37 says of the people who heard:

Now when they heard this, they were pricked in their heart, and said unto Peter and to the rest of the apostles, Men and brethren, what shall we do?

Peter's response was simple:

Then Peter said unto them, Repent, and be baptized every one of you in the name of Jesus Christ for the remission of sins, and ye shall receive the gift of the Holy Ghost.

For the promise is unto you, and to your children, and to all that are afar off, even as many as the Lord our God shall call.

Acts 2:38,39

In this scripture passage we find the New Testament promise of God to all those who will heed His instructions:

1. Repent — the witness of the blood.

2. *Be baptized* — water baptism as a sign of cleansing from sin.
3. *Receive the Holy Ghost* — the evidence of the Spirit.

Who is this promise for?

When Peter was speaking to these people, he said, *For the promise is unto you, and to your children.* The promise had already passed beyond the apostles to those people there before him, then on to their children. But that is not all Peter said. He continued with these important words: *... and to all that are afar off, even as many as the Lord our God shall call.* That's you and me!

On the day of Pentecost we have the direct promise that what God did at that moment He would never cease to do. The promise was for them, for their children, for all those afar off, even as many as God would call.

Since the call of God is the call to repentance, as long as God is saving people, He will also be filling them with His precious Holy Spirit.

Charismatics today provide the footings in the Body of Christ for what God began 2,000 years ago. We are living in that glorious moment prophesied by Joel:

I will pour out my spirit upon all flesh; and your sons and your daughters shall prophesy, your old men shall dream dreams, your young men shall see visions:

And also upon the servants and upon the handmaids in those days will I pour out my spirit.

Joel 2:28,29

28

In the Body of Christ today we have the old, the young, and the middle-aged, which is the way it ought to be.

Fruit of the Charismatic Blessing

The charismatic experience, the charisma, has certain benefits and blessings that accompany it.

Love of God's Word

There comes into your life a love for the Word of God that you have never before experienced. The Bible, which seemed to you like a dead book of religious history, suddenly comes alive and seems more relevant than the morning news.

Stewardship

Another fruit of this charisma is a level of stewardship previously unknown. I have found the charismatics to be a remarkable people of stewardship. Throughout the world it is the same. The more they give, the more God gives.

Facing Up To Sin

A third fruit of the charismatic experience is the ability to face up to sin and to confess it. So many religious people try to hide from their sins by making excuses for their behavior. No people in the world face up to reality like the charismatics. If there is sin in their lives, they just come out with it and say, "I'm sorry." Then they receive their forgiveness and become cleansed.

Evangelistic Compassion

Another fruit of the charismatic way is a tremendous growth in evangelistic compassion for others. You will not find another people who love so deeply and so wonderfully as the charismatics — the people who have become identified with the gifts of the Holy Spirit. These people of evangelistic compassion will go throughout the world, teaching and preaching the Gospel because it is in their hearts to do so.

Reaching Out To Others

Another fruit of the charisma is special ministry and service to people in the field of counseling. Charismatics are free to talk to people and help them, because they have a spirit of counseling. They know what to say and how to help those in need.

Joy and Happiness

Charismatics are a singing people, and singing will do special things for you. The Bible says, *A merry heart doeth good like a medicine* (Prov. 17:22). There is a spirit inside charismatics that says, *Rejoice in the Lord alway: and again I say, Rejoice* (Phil. 4:4). The move of God is evident today by the joy in our hearts, the melody that is within us.

Physical Healing

If you want to hear many outstanding experiences in healing, spend some time with people who are filled with the Spirit of God. You will hear testimonies of healings like you have never heard before.

3
Sign Gifts of the Holy Spirit

The *charisma* is a spiritual phenomenon, unique to our time, one which has been met with tremendous response by millions of people throughout the world.

The word *charisma* is a Greek word which means "spiritual gift" — not natural or carnal or "soulical," but spiritual — freely given to us by God. In its characteristic usage *charisma* denotes an *extraordinary ability that is bestowed upon a human being by the infinite strength and power of the Third Person of the Trinity, Who is called the Holy Ghost.* This spiritual gift is bestowed as a special service to the Body of Christ.

These gifts from God to the local church are what we call "sign gifts." They are supernatural endowments that God places within our lives. The Third Person of the Trinity is the Governor Who brings them in, situates them, chooses which we shall have, and lets them flow out through us into the world.

Regarding the living body of the New Testament Church in these last days, Jesus Christ says: *And the gates of hell shall not prevail against it* (Matt. 16:18). We have come to the titanic contest between good and evil. For us to be the kind of people God wants in these trying times, we must have the gifts of the Spirit. It is imperative that we be qualified spiritually — that we know about spiritual gifts, understand them, and be able to use them wisely as the Lord wills.

These charisma gifts of the Spirit are the weapons of our warfare. If we have these gifts

31

functioning within us, they become our battle axes, our guns, our swords, our spears — all the artillery we need to destroy the works and the powers of the Devil.

The gifts of the Spirit are not tender little gifts. They are dynamic, dangerous, warlike. You will understand this more as we get into our study and show, in particular, how the gifts have functioned in the Word of God and how they still function today.

These are the special weapons that you will be able to handle dexterously. Some people will not understand you and may call you a fanatic, but that might not be such a bad word after all. In my hometown of South Bend, Indiana, we have great "fanatics." They are Notre Dame "fanatics," or "fans," which only means they get excited about the football games. You and I are also "fans" — fans of the Lord Jesus Christ. We get excited about Him, and we don't mind saying so!

The gifts of the Spirit are the weapons God gives us to fight and win our battles. We must never underestimate their strength, their power, and their usefulness; but we must study them deeply and continuously until they function through us. First, we learn of their existence and we say, "Lord, thank You for the knowledge we have." Then we learn how to avail ourselves of them. Next, we learn about their proper usage. In some bodies of believers, the gifts of the Spirit are misused; and misuse of the gifts will only cause them to cease functioning.

In this study I want to provide you with a firm foundation on the work of the Holy Spirit. I want you to be able to answer any question about spiritual gifts; but more than just explain them to people, I want you to put them into operation both in your personal life and in the local body where you worship. These spiritual gifts should function through you with great wisdom, so that God is pleased with you.

Spiritual gifts are not the icing on the cake or the meringue on the pie; they are the weapons of our warfare. The gifts of the Spirit are not designed just to make you different from other people. They are given to equip you for God's service.

Many people say they would like to have God's power and God's gifts, so they can sit down in a rocking chair and rock themselves right into eternity. But God will not give you the weapons of His warfare so that you can sit in a rocking chair. As long as you are in a rocking chair, you have no need of the gifts.

Spiritual gifts spring up mightily out in the highways and byways — out where the people are. Look at the life of Jesus. The gifts of the Spirit came into operation when He faced the people, such as the Gadarene demoniac. (Luke 8:26-36.) That was a very frightening situation. When Jesus met certain situations, He had to know things that normally could not be known by the physical eyes or ears; a spiritual phenomenon had to take place.

If you desire the gifts of the Spirit to function in your life, you must be a person of action. You must say, "I am ready for the battlefield. I am ready for God's weapons to function in my life."

The charismatic move of God today is the hope of the Church. It is absolutely necessary to God's plan for the world.

There was a great outcry several years ago, proclaiming, *God is dead!* The move of God today is His answer to that statement. God is very much alive, and He is alive within us! He is alive right now, doing just as much for the Church today as ever before.

We can receive the same gifts today that the infant Church received in the first century. We can visualize that New Testament army of God as it moved across the world, and we can expect God to do the same in His Church today.

4

Two Foundation Stones

Perhaps the greatest thing about the gifts of the Spirit are the two foundation stones on which they are laid: *unity and love*. If the gifts of the Spirit are to function in any church body, these two elements must be present.

The Apostle Paul explained the need for unity and love in his first epistle to the Corinthian church.

The twelfth chapter deals with unity in the Body of Christ. It takes an entire chapter to reveal how important it is for you to have, not just a nose, but a nose and an ear; not just an arm, but an arm and a leg. The Body of Christ is one complete structure, and there must be unity. I am not better than you; you are not better than me. We are one together in the Lord Jesus Christ.

The thirteenth chapter drives home the most important point of all: There must be love, pure love. Without it, the spiritual gifts cannot function.

In studying the nine spiritual gifts from 1 Corinthians, chapters 12-14, it would be best to ignore the chapter divisions. Paul wrote this epistle as a continuous letter. There were no chapters. If you would read it with that in mind, you would see that what we view as chapter 13 is not specifically a dissertation on love, but an amplification of the gifts of the Spirit.

Unity

There must be unity in the Body of Christ.

The gifts of the Spirit will not function long without unity. On the day of Pentecost — the day the

Church was born — the people were all together in one place and in one accord, not divided or separated. The Church was born in unity, and the Church can only be great in unity.

In years past, there have been celebrity evangelists who possessed certain spiritual gifts, but they seemed to function and operate as separate entities. Thirty or forty years ago there were some great manifestations of the gifts of the Spirit in America, but I am ashamed to say that the people through whom these gifts functioned pulled away from the Body. Some began to call themselves by such names as "God's man of the hour." The gifts then were not identified with the Body of Christ, but only with a person. That cannot be.

I am discovering more each day that God is "Body-conscious." By that, I mean He sees us continually as one Body — the Body of Christ. You and I, as members of that Body, must learn to flow together. I am not one thing and you another; we are one together. For the gifts of the Spirit to flow as they should, it must be through the Body, which is the Church.

God is ready for these gifts to function through the total Body, without a great emphasis upon any one individual. Each of us should feel that we are chosen of God. No one who is being used of the Holy Spirit is unique in himself; he is only unique in that he is permitted to be a part of the Body. All of us are part of Christ's glorious Body! Today we are entering that time of unity, and I am so thankful for it. We are becoming the same size, where there are no little ones or big ones — just everyone flowing together in the gifts of the Holy Spirit.

In 1 Corinthians, chapter 12, we see this unity of the Body described:

Now concerning spiritual gifts, brethren, I would not have you ignorant . . .

Now there are diversities of gifts, but the same Spirit.

And there are differences of administrations, but the same Lord.

And there are diversities of operations, but it is the same God which worketh all in all.

1 Corinthians 12:1,4-6

Diversities of Gifts

Within the nine gifts of the Spirit, there are three groups: revelation, power, and inspiration. There are diversities of gifts, but all three groups flow from only one Source: the Holy Spirit of God.

Differences of Administrations

What does this mean? Let me give you an example.

It may cost Dr. Billy Graham $50 million to run his evangelistic association for a whole year, while a little country preacher may not pay more than $500 a year. What is the difference? Their administrations are not the same. Billy Graham reaches out to millions of people. A little country preacher may not reach more than fifty people during an entire year.

There may be differences of administrations, but always remember, it is the same Lord. That means we should neither look down on anybody nor look up to anybody. All of us are functioning for the same reason under the guidance and direction of the same Lord.

We are not to exalt persons, no matter who they are. We are to exalt Jesus. No matter what size the administration might be, there is only one Lord — the same Lord Who does both the little things and the big things. We must not despise one and praise another. We must say, "Thanks be unto the Lord for all the wonderful works He does on the face of this earth!"

Diversities of Operations

Different ministries go about their tasks in different ways. Some reach out via television; others, via radio; still others, via the printed page. Some are involved in all three. Yet many others confine themselves to direct personal contact with the people, face-to-face and eye-to-eye.

Again, you must never forget: No matter what type of operation is being used, *it is the same God which worketh all in all.*

You may say, "The Lord must not be with me. I'm not doing much." If you have brought even one soul to Jesus, that is worth the whole world.

We must stop exalting or debasing, looking up or looking down. We must look forward by the power of the Holy Spirit into the great harvest fields. Then God can use us and bless us. These gifts of the Spirit will not function until we form the right attitude in our souls. There are diversities of operations, big and little, but it is the same God Who works in all of them.

The Gifts Bring Profit

But the manifestation of the Spirit is given to every man to profit withal.

1 Corinthians 12:7

To manifest means "to show." This flowing out of these gifts of the Spirit is given *to every man.* Some people have developed a philosophy that in every church body there should be only one or two people who operate in spiritual gifts. That cannot be found in the Bible. God wants each of us to have the gifts of the Spirit functioning in our lives.

The manifestation of the Spirit is given to every man to profit withal. When God gives you something, it is a good thing. It is a plus, not a minus, and there is profit behind it.

No church body ever decreased when the gifts of the Spirit were in operation there.

No person ever became weaker when the gifts of the Spirit held a dominant role in his life. These gifts always bring a profit. Your assets are better when you get the gifts of the Spirit working. God wants the gifts of the Spirit to function in your life. He wants you to profit and He wants the Body of Christ to profit.

First Corinthians 12:8-10 lists the nine gifts of the Spirit:

For to one is given by the Spirit the word of wisdom; to another the word of knowledge by the same Spirit;

To another faith by the same Spirit; to another the gifts of healing by the same Spirit;

To another the working of miracles; to another prophecy; to another discerning of spirits; to another

39

divers kinds of tongues; to another the interpretation of tongues.

Then in verse 11 we again see the thought that was conveyed in verse 7:

But all these worketh that one and the selfsame Spirit, dividing to every man severally as he will.

To every man — God said it twice in just these few verses. . . . *dividing to every man severally* . . . . That means you need not stop with one or two; you can receive several of them.

Then there is a small qualification: . . . *as he will.* The Holy Spirit has something to do with it. He knows your capacity. He knows how you would use the gifts. Therefore, He gives them *as He wills.*

One Body Together

In verse 12 there is another admonition for unity: *For as the body* (human body) *is one, and hath many members* (collectively), *and all the members of that one body, being many, are one body: so also is Christ.*

The Lord is pleading through the Apostle Paul for unity in the Body of Christ. For many hundreds of years it has grieved the Lord and made the Devil to laugh whenever we as children of the Lord fight among ourselves. I pray the Lord will never permit me to fight with another Christian as long as I live. When I discern a fight in the works, I seek with all my heart to back off.

God's people should not fight with one another over doctrines and denominational differences. We are bound together neither by denominations nor by doctrines, but by the shed blood of the Lord Jesus Christ. We are blood brothers, born again of His

Spirit and by His blood. Any person who has been born again is your brother or sister, no matter what their denominational tag may be. If a person belongs to Jesus, he belongs to you, too. Both of you are the Body of Christ. If he draws a circle and leaves you out, you should draw a bigger one and take him in!

Strength In Unity

For by one Spirit (the Holy Ghost) are we all baptized into one body, whether we be Jews (the religious people) or Gentiles (the non-religious people), whether we be bond or free; and have been all made to drink into one Spirit.

1 Corinthians 12:13

There is a strength and a force in unity that will not be found any other place. The unity of the Body of Christ is like none other.

Once the Church of Jesus Christ comes together and flows as one colossal Body, the power and love of God will spread throughout the whole world.

For the body is not one member, but many.

If the foot shall say, Because I am not the hand, I am not of the body; is it therefore not of the body?

And if the ear shall say, Because I am not the eye, I am not of the body; is it therefore not of the body?

If the whole body were an eye, where were the hearing? If the whole were the hearing, where were the smelling?

But now hath God set the members every one of them in the body, as it hath pleased him.

1 Corinthians 12:14-18

41

You may not like being an ear and may want to be a nose; but if God made you an ear, be a good one. Keep yourself open to hear.

If God has made you a toe, walk well. Be a support for the foot, because that is what God has called you to do.

Chosen By God

I believe the Lord chooses just the right place for each of us to fill in the Body. God needs all kinds of people to appeal to all kinds of people. We must recognize the total Body and determine to flow together in Him. I think perhaps there is nothing more dynamic in the world than to be placed in the Body of Christ *by Him.*

When I started off to go around the world as a missionary at 20 years of age, I had only $12 in my pocket. As I began to weep, the Lord said, "Read John 15:16." So I turned to it: *Ye have not chosen me, but I have chosen you.* Then I realized a great truth: It was not *my* decision to be a missionary and travel around the world. The Lord had made the decision for me. All I had to do was agree to do what God had asked of me. What a relief!

How beautiful it is when God sets us in the Body! If God has called you to be a businessman, stay right where you are and be a good one. You are needed in that position. God put you there for a purpose. If you are a housewife, be the greatest there is. If God has planted you in the ministry, then be an effective minister, in Jesus' name!

Wherever God has put you, just be strong. You have no idea how many lives you will touch and bless and strengthen in the place God has put you. You are what you are because God made you that way. It was not by accident.

There Must Be Unity

If they were all one member, where were the body? But now are they many members, yet but one body.

And the eye cannot say unto the hand, I have no need of thee: nor again the head to the feet, I have no need of you.

Nay, much more those members of the body, which seem to be more feeble, are necessary.

1 Corinthians 12:19-22

Why would God use language like this to speak of the gifts of the Spirit? To show us with clarity the need for unity. In order for these nine spiritual gifts to function in the Body, there must be unity.

If you are contrary to the unity of the Body, you cannot expect these gifts to operate in your life. The beginning of the knowledge of these gifts is knowing they are in the Body in the unity of the Spirit. We will see this flow as we honor one another, appreciate one another, and lift up one another.

You are a candidate for these mighty gifts of the Holy Spirit to function in your heart and in your life. God wants His people to operate in His power. Nothing is so powerful as an idea whose time has come, and I believe the time has come now for these gifts to flow. That is why it is so necessary for the Body of Christ to have teaching in this area. We must not go astray. We must not misuse what God has provided. As long as we keep the gifts in the place God wants them, they will function today just as they did in the Acts of the Apostles.

43

Nay, much more those members of the body, which seem to be more feeble, are necessary:

And those members of the body, which we think to be less honourable, upon these we bestow more abundant honour; and our uncomely parts have more abundant comeliness.

For our comely parts have no need: but God hath tempered the body together, having given more abundant honour to that part which lacked:

That there should be no schism in the body; but that the members should have the same care one for another.

And whether one member suffer, all the members suffer with it; or one member be honoured, all the members rejoice with it.

1 Corinthians 12:22-26

The word *schism* (v. 25) is important. It means a division or separation. God does not want a schism in the Church. He does not want us fighting with one another. When a person comes to you grumbling or finding fault with another person, don't even argue with him. The best way to put a stop to it is by saying: "Why don't we pray about that situation? God will take care of it for you."

It is the beginning of the moving of God's power among us when we start caring one for another, really caring. There should be a real spiritual relationship among God's people.

It is so easy to become selfish and isolated, to separate ourselves when God wants us to flow in the Body. You cannot see yourself as a separate entity. You cannot go off into a corner and say, "Look at me. I'm really great!" No, you are not great. God is great;

Jesus is great; *the Holy Spirit is great!* You are what you are because of what God did for you through Jesus.

Now ye are the body of Christ, and members in particular.

God hath set some in the church, first apostles, secondarily prophets, thirdly teachers, after that miracles, then gifts of healings, helps, governments, diversities of tongues.

Are all apostles? are all prophets? are all teachers? are all workers of miracles?

Have all the gifts of healing? do all speak with tongues? do all interpret?

1 Corinthians 12:27-30

The answer to each of these questions is a very definite, "NO!"

The key verse in this entire passage of Scripture is verse 31: *But covet earnestly the best gifts* . . . .

The word "covet" is a strong word. When used in the carnal sense, it is wrong; we are not to covet our neighbor's goods. (Ex. 20:17.) But coveting between you and God is different.

You will not receive the gifts of the Spirit by accident. You will receive the gifts of the Spirit only because your desire is so intense that you *must* have them; then you will receive them.

But covet earnestly the best gifts: and yet shew I unto you a more excellent way. This "more excellent way" is the second foundation stone on which the operation of the gifts of the Spirit is based: love.

Love

The goal of the New Testament Church is to sweep the world with the power of God, but it cannot

45

be done without love. Love is the key that unlocks the door to all God has for us today.

Let's look at what the Apostle Paul has to say about love in 1 Corinthians, chapter 13. In the first three verses, various spiritual gifts are enumerated. However, we are told that without love, these gifts will add up to nothing.

Though I speak with the tongues of men and of angels, and have not love, I am become as sounding brass, or a tinkling cymbal.

And though I have the gift of prophecy, and understand all mysteries, and all knowledge; and though I have all faith, so that I could remove mountains, and have not love, I am nothing.

And though I bestow all my goods to feed the poor, and though I give my body to be burned, and have not love, it profiteth me nothing.

1 Corinthians 13:1-3

Paul is saying here that without love, you cannot produce the gifts of the Spirit. You cannot produce them in an atmosphere of selfishness and jealousy; they just will not function.

You may have a million-dollar cathedral, but without love you are nothing.

Your minister may be the finest orator in the world, but without love he is nothing.

Your choir may be the finest choir anywhere on earth, but without love it is nothing.

Your congregation may include the finest, most respectable people in the city, but without love they are nothing.

You may be able to raise the dead in your ministry, but without love you are nothing.

Then in verses 4-8 we are told what love is:

Love is that force within you which suffers a long time, and is kind and gracious.

Love is that force within you that does not envy. Another person may have more than you have, but it doesn't matter. His car may be nicer than your car, his home nicer than your home, but you are not envious.

Love does not promote itself.

Love is not puffed up, making a big "I" and a little "u."

Love does not behave itself unseemly or inappropriately. It always acts the right way.

Love does not seek her own, is not easily provoked, and thinks no evil.

Love does not rejoice in iniquity, but rejoices in the truth.

Love bears all things, believes all things, hopes in all things, and endures all things.

Love never fails!

Then verse 13 says: *And now abideth faith, hope, love, these three; but the greatest of these is love.*

5
Weapons of Our Warfare

I make the following statement without qualification because I believe it with all my heart: The greatest unused energy in the world today cannot be found under the ground with the oil and coal resources; that latent power is within the Church of the Lord Jesus Christ.

The power of God is invincible, and the gifts of the Spirit have been given to the Church as the weapons of our warfare. However, the Church today is going into battle without a true knowledge of those weapons. Any time you go to battle without your weapons properly functioning, you cannot expect to win the fight.

It is my true desire that through this study of the gifts of the Spirit, you will recognize the true greatness of these spiritual gifts and allow them to become a vital part of your life.

When our Lord Jesus came to this earth to conquer it and redeem it, He functioned only within the framework of the gifts of the Spirit. His total ministry on earth was not as God, but as a man, functioning in the gifts of the Spirit. All the "miracles" Jesus performed were the result of a gift of the Spirit functioning at that time.

Do you believe that Jesus always told the truth? He did! Then let me remind you of what He said in John 14:12: *He that believeth on me, the works that I do shall he do also; and greater works than these shall he do; because I go unto my Father.* The ministry Jesus performed on this earth was directed, guided, and energized by the Holy Spirit — the same

Holy Spirit that you and I have today. We can expect to do the same works Jesus did if we will follow, line upon line and precept upon precept, everything the Word of God teaches.

Each one of us has a right to every gift of the Holy Spirit, without exception. Each believer in Christ has the right to any and every gift of the Spirit. When we leave ourselves out, it is through unbelief. We say, "That is for someone else. It can't be for me." But the gifts *are* for you! They are provided for the total Body of Christ, and you as a believer are a part of His Body.

It is time to cry out, O ye Church of the Lord Jesus Christ! Put on the whole armor of God! Clothe yourself in the gifts of the Spirit! Go out against the enemy and destroy him! Bring to the Kingdom of God glory and majesty because He is the King of kings and the Lord of lords! You and I should see victories every day, and never know defeat!

Jesus said that if you wish to take a prey, you must first bind the strong man. (Matt. 12:29.) When we seek to take a prey in a pagan land, such as Tibet or India, it is imperative that we use the weapons of our warfare. Not to do so is to suffer humiliating defeat at the hands of witchcraft, superstition, and heathen religion. Only when that pagan darkness is pushed back can we know true victory.

Zechariah 4:6 says it is *not by might* (or organization), *nor by power* (or a decision of a board), *but by my spirit, saith the Lord of hosts.*

We can reach out today to save the world in which we live, but it will never be done by organizational strength or even by the strength of numbers. God can win a mighty battle with just a few people. By using only Gideon and his faithful 300, God took care of tens of thousands of the enemy. (Judg. 7 and 8.)

God does not need a host of men to win a battle; He just needs sincere and dedicated people, whose hearts are fully turned to Him. In this case, to win a total victory He needs those who have received the endowment of the gifts of the Spirit to function in their lives and ministries.

The Body of Christ is an advancing army; we do not retreat. We have total victory; we do not know defeat. Our warfare is not carnal; it is spiritual. We are not fighting doctrines or people or denominations. We are warring in the spirit, and the gifts of the Spirit are a necessary part of our fighting gear, both defensive and offensive, but especially offensive. It is the power of God flowing from our spirits which convinces people.

I believe we are living in a prophetic moment. Jesus Christ will soon be returning for His Church, and He does not want to come back for a Church that is sick and sad and defeated. He wants to come back for a Church that is glorious — winning victory after victory and setting men free by the power of God.

6
God's Gifts to the Church

The gifts of the Spirit cannot be earned. They are called "gifts" to reveal that there is only one way to obtain them: They are given to the Church by God. However, this by no means minimizes their importance.

These gifts are not optional. The people of the Church have missed God in the past by deciding for themselves whether or not they would accept them. The gifts of the Spirit are not placed at the disposal of the Church on a take-it-or-leave-it proposition. We either take them or lose what we have.

Categories of Gifts

The gifts of the Spirit are divine communications, transmitted from the Holy Trinity through the channel of the Holy Spirit, the Third Person of the Trinity, into the Church — the Body of the Lord Jesus Christ upon the earth.

The number of divine perfection is 3. Everything in the universe that is stamped with perfection is stamped with that 3.

There is the threefold nature of God: Father, Son, and Holy Ghost. *For there are three that bear record in heaven, the Father, the Word, and the Holy Ghost: and these three are one* (1 John 5:7).

There is the threefold nature of man: spirit, soul, and body. *And the very God of peace sanctify you wholly; and I pray God your whole spirit and soul and body be preserved blameless unto the coming of our Lord Jesus Christ* (1 Thess. 5:23).

You will notice as well the mark of divine perfection in the gifts of the Spirit. They divide themselves naturally and spiritually into 3 primary categories: revelation, power, and inspiration. Within each of the 3 categories, there are 3 sub-groups.

So you have 3 + 3 + 3. Perfection x Perfection, or Perfection + Perfection + Perfection.

No matter how you choose to look at it, that is absolute perfection.

Each category is distinguished from the others by the work God is doing through it. In each category He is doing something separate and distinct from the others. It is through these three vast areas — revelation, power (or energy), and inspiration — that the Church of Jesus Christ becomes an invincible force, stronger than any power known on the face of the earth.

Revelation Gifts

Through this prime category — the revelation gifts — the infinite God, Creator of the universe, is revealing His truth to man. There is a revelation from heaven of certain facts which man could not know by way of his physical senses. It would have to be a miracle; man would have no way of knowing except by divine revelation.

We see an example of this in Matthew 16:16,17: *Simon Peter answered and said, Thou art the Christ, the Son of the living God. And Jesus answered and said unto him, Blessed art thou, Simon Bar-jona: for flesh and blood hath not revealed it unto thee, but my Father which is in heaven.*

Within this category there is the word of wisdom, the word of knowledge, and the discerning of spirits.

Power Gifts

In the second category of spiritual gifts — the power gifts — God imparts His own divine powers and abilities to man. The gifts of power involve a supernatural ability and energy which man does not naturally possess.

This category of power gifts includes the gift of faith, the gifts of healing, and the working of miracles. Within this group is found the only gift which has plurality: the gifts of healing. We will explain later why it is in the plural form.

Many of these gifts are like a chain. Each is linked together with others in such a way that when you pull one, you are pulling the whole load. Sometimes it is difficult to divide the links and distinguish between them because they are so interrelated. We see this especially in the gifts of power because both the gift of faith and the working of miracles are operating in the supernatural.

Inspiration Gifts

The third category of the gifts of the Spirit is inspiration. In the gifts of inspiration God brings His anointing and His blessing to the Church.

This category includes the gift of prophecy, the gift of tongues, and the interpretation of tongues. These gifts have to do with corporate worship, not with personal worship.

First Corinthians 14:3 gives the total blessing of these gifts of inspiration: edification, exhortation, and comfort. These three gifts which come to us through inspiration are the three most needed ministries in the Church of the Lord Jesus Christ.

Each Gift Defined

The nine gifts of the Spirit are as distinct as the seven lamps of the golden lampstand in the temple in Jerusalem and as individual as the nine fruit of the Spirit that blossom in our lives. Yet they are so linked and interlinked by the Holy Spirit that it is sometimes difficult to determine exactly which gift is in manifestation. At times there might be the working of miracles; at other times the gifts of healing.

For this reason I admonish you to avoid a heavy emphasis on definitions. Definitions can cause separation among the people. The Devil would love to have us quarrel over definitions. Arguments can arise between two people who actually believe the same thing but are defining it differently.

Let's be careful to be courteous and remain in love. How a person is healed — whether through the working of miracles, the gifts of healing, or the gift of faith — really is not the issue. The important thing is that he is healed!

The following are brief one-sentence definitions of each gift of the Holy Spirit:

The word of wisdom is the revealing of the prophetic future under the anointing of God. In the Old Testament every seer and every prophet who foretold the future was endowed with this gift. A word of God's wisdom is just that: *a word.* When God gives you a word of His wisdom, He gives only a fragment. The same is true with the word of knowledge.

The word of knowledge is the revealing of a fact in existence which can only be supernaturally revealed. It cannot be seen or heard or known naturally.

This is the difference between the word of knowledge and the word of wisdom: The word of knowledge is a revelation of a fact that exists; the word of wisdom is a revelation of the future. Daniel was operating in the word of wisdom when he said there would be a Persian empire, a Grecian empire, and a Roman empire. At that time those empires had not been born.

The discerning of spirits has to do with the comprehending of the human spirit, supernaturally revealed by the Holy Ghost. It is not the discerning of demons, but the discerning of the human spirit — good and bad. With this gift, you can look straight through a person and know whether or not he is telling the truth.

The gift of faith is God's bringing to pass a supernatural change. No human effort is involved.

On the other hand, the gift of *the working of miracles* does work through a human instrument. It is a person doing a supernatural act by the divine energy of the Holy Spirit. An excellent example is Samson bare-handedly killing a lion. That was a miracle.

In *the gifts of healing* God supernaturally heals the sick through a ministry anointed by the Holy Spirit. A person is given by the Spirit of God a gift to pray for a particular kind of sickness or disease. Remember, there are many ways to be healed. This includes only a small portion of them. There might be as many gifts as there are diseases. This is why the term is in the plural form.

The gift of tongues is the ministry of proclaiming in a public meeting a message from God in a language not understood by the person giving it. Because he has not studied that language and does not know it, he does not give it from his mind, but from his spirit.

When a message in tongues has been given, then *the interpretation of tongues* goes into operation. Without any mental faculties being involved, the message that has been given in another language is interpreted supernaturally by the Holy Spirit through another person.

The gift of prophecy is the anointed speaking forth of words of edification, exhortation, and comfort — words supernaturally given to the Church from God.

7
The Revelation Gifts

There are three gifts of revelation: the word of wisdom, the word of knowledge, and the discerning of spirits. In these three revelation gifts, God reveals information supernaturally to a man or woman — information which comes from outside the bounds of that person's natural processes; information which their minds did not conceive, their ears did not hear, and their eyes did not see.

The Word of Wisdom

The gift of the word of wisdom is a supernatural revelation of the divine purposes of God. It is a divine communication, a message to the Church from God, given by the Holy Spirit through a believer.

In the gift of the word of God's wisdom, God gives forth a small segment or portion of information from His vast storehouse of wisdom. Wisdom has to do with that which is unborn, or of the future. When God gives a word of His wisdom, He is revealing something that has not yet come to pass. Every prophet in the Bible possessed this gift, and prophets who live today also possess it.

This gift unveils, in part, the purposes of God on the earth. The Apostle Paul explains it this way: *But we speak the wisdom of God in a mystery, even the hidden wisdom, which God ordained before the world unto our glory* (1 Cor. 2:7). The word of wisdom involves speaking the hidden things — things we would not normally or naturally know.

Remember, this is not just the gift of wisdom; it is the *word* of wisdom. It is a fragment of the total wisdom of God, just as a word is a fragment of a sentence. The word of wisdom is a part or portion of the great omniscience of God.

It is very difficult for us as human beings to realize that God is all-wise — that He knows the total past, the total present, and the total future, all at one time. When He conveys to the Church through one of His servants a word of wisdom, He has made that person wise in that one matter, but not wise concerning all things. When a person receives the gift of the word of wisdom, he does not suddenly become a "know-it-all." The word of wisdom has no relation to a person's natural knowledge. Whether a person has achieved brilliant academic success has nothing to do with this gift. A person with very little education can operate it just as well.

This gift of the word of wisdom can transform the world in which we live today. It can fascinate this world. The Devil has a counterfeit for everything God has. These people who claim to read the future are counterfeiting what God wants to do through His people in the earth. God wants you to know the future. It is time for this gift to function in a way that it has never functioned before in the history of the world.

If the Church was moving in the spiritual gifts of revelation — the word of wisdom, the word of knowledge, and the discerning of spirits — there would be no need for fortune-tellers, crystal ball-gazers, Ouija boards, tea-leaf readers, palm readers, and all the other paraphernalia that the Devil uses to deceive the people of our generation. We are engulfed in the greatest wave of black magic and witchcraft this country has ever known. One reason for this is that the Church has not properly operated in the gifts of the Spirit. We have not used the weapons of our warfare to stop the Devil's counterfeits.

I challenge you to seek God for these major gifts. As 1 Corinthians 12:31 says, we are to *covet earnestly the best gifts.* If we will do that — and seek them with all our hearts — we will find that they are available to us.

Through the gift of the word of God's wisdom, God makes you wise to the future and you know what is going to take place. Rather than worry about it or work at making it come to pass, you merely let it function, and it happens exactly as God has told you.

In the Acts of the Apostles we see these gifts functioning time and time again. If they functioned in the early Church, they should function in today's Church; and they *will* function today if we will desire it. God wants us to have it.

Revelation Gifts in the Old Testament

There are some very remarkable men in the Old Testament who had the gifts of the Spirit functioning in their lives. The power that motivated these remarkable Old Testament ministries — men like Noah, Ezekiel, Daniel, David, Joel, and Isaiah — is the same power that motivates us today: the power of the Holy Spirit.

God is not doing something special through the operation of spiritual gifts today. He has always worked this way, and He always will. By harnessing these powers and utilizing them as God desires, we can change the world in which we live.

God wants to motivate us by the same gifts of the Spirit that He used to motivate all those men of the Old Testament. They were not just select individuals — special people in whose footsteps no ordinary Christian could hope to follow. All that they did — the works that are recorded in the divine record — is available to us today. We should expect the gifts of the Spirit to function in our lives just as they did during Old Testament times.

Word of Wisdom in the Old Testament

All the prophets of the Bible were endowed with the spiritual gift of wisdom. They were seers of the future, making known God's wisdom about that which would come to pass. Here are some examples:

Noah

In Genesis 6:12,13 God revealed to Noah the coming of the Flood:

God looked upon the earth, and, behold, it was corrupt; for all flesh had corrupted his way upon the earth.

And God said unto Noah, The end of all flesh is come before me; for the earth is filled with violence through them; and, behold, I will destroy them with the earth.

Noah knew for a hundred and twenty years that God would destroy the earth. This is the gift of the word of God's wisdom functioning in Noah. He received only a word of what God was going to do.

Daniel

The prophet Daniel had great visions. He saw empires leap into existence and perform on the stage of human history. Before they were ever born, he named the very nature these empires would have: lions and bears and leopards and beasts. It was the gift of the word of wisdom in operation that caused him to know these things.

Ezekiel

The prophet Ezekiel very dramatically foretold the whole future, as we see it in Ezekiel, chapters 38 and 39. This demonstrates how God reveals the future. Every day we get nearer to the fulfillment of that word of God's wisdom.

He said that from the north there would come an army against the country of unwalled villages. In Ezekiel's day there was no such thing as an unwalled village; they did not exist. The towns needed walls for protection against wild animals and enemies. Today there is not one village in Israel with a wall around it. Also, there had never been a real threat to Israel from the north parts before Russia took her place there as a world empire.

That is a word of God's wisdom. God told Ezekiel exactly what would happen. When we see these things coming to pass, we should rejoice. These are the words of God's wisdom being fulfilled before our very eyes.

David

David revealed through the Psalms how the Messiah would come and how He would die. It was a revelation of the future as seen, for example, in Psalms 2 and 22.

Joel

When the prophet Joel prophesied that in the last days God's Spirit would be poured out upon all flesh, he was revealing the future. A word of God's wisdom was being brought forth.

Isaiah

Chapter 53 of Isaiah is one of the greatest prophecies in the Bible. The great prophet Isaiah described the nature of the Messiah. He described all the ways He would die, what kind of person He would be, and what His death would mean to us. He even wrote that by His stripes we would be healed. In Isaiah's day stripes were not known as a form of punishment. This was the word of God's wisdom functioning through Isaiah.

Word of Wisdom in the New Testament

Foremost among those demonstrating the word of wisdom in the New Testament was the ministry of the Lord Jesus Christ.

In Matthew 24, Luke 21, and Mark 13, Christ foretold the destruction of the temple in Jerusalem, which came a few years later, and the signs which would accompany His return to earth for His Church. Many of these things are coming to pass in our generation. Some of them have yet to come to pass. All of this is what the word of God's wisdom is — a revelation of the future.

The New Testament is filled with instances of the gift of the word of wisdom being manifested. In several epistles to the Church, the Apostle Paul revealed things that would come to pass in the last days. The Apostle Peter was very emphatic about signs that would come to pass before the Lord Jesus returned. The word of wisdom functioned through these men just as it did through the Old Testament prophets.

An example of this gift functioning for the Apostle Paul is related in Acts, chapter 23, when Paul almost lost his life at the hands of an angry Jewish mob. When it looked as if he would die, the Lord spoke to him by the word of wisdom and said: *Be of good cheer, Paul: for as thou hast testified of me in Jerusalem, so must thou bear witness also at Rome* (Acts 23:11). Paul had no way of knowing he would ever speak for God in Rome, but God revealed the future to him. That was the word of God's wisdom.

How Wisdom Is Manifested

The Holy Spirit can convey the word of wisdom in many ways.

To Joseph it was the *interpreting of a dream* of the future. When Joseph was 17 years old, God showed him his whole life — that he would be a great leader and even his own brothers would bow down before him. No one believed it, but it came to pass.

Daniel received wisdom by *a night vision*. It was the word of wisdom projected into the future.

Ezekiel was *caught away into the Spirit* for a revelation.

The Apostle John was *caught up in the Spirit* on the Lord's day, and the entire book of Revelation flashed before him.

God has no set way of dealing with the problems of this world. He unveils hidden mysteries and the wisdom to execute His counsels in the way He considers best at that time.

Many times we think Jesus can do things only one way, but that is not true. The same is true with the word of wisdom. It does not have to function the same way each time. It can function as a dream or a vision. You could even be caught up into the third heaven as Paul was. God has many ways to do things. He can work with you in a unique way — a way He has not operated before. He can do whatever He wants to do.

Prophecy vs. Word of Wisdom

A clear distinction must be formed in our minds regarding the simple inspirational gift of prophecy in the New Testament and the word of wisdom.

First Corinthians 14:3 gives the full measure of the blessings of prophecy. There is no element of revelation associated with it. *He that prophesieth speaketh unto men to edification, and exhortation, and comfort.*

Any person who speaks out in church, foretelling the future, has left this simple gift of prophecy — the least of the gifts — and has moved into the greatest and foremost revelation gift — the word of wisdom — whereby he foresees the future. The prophet of either the Old Testament or the New Testament is a seer. He sees into the future and possesses the gift of the word of God's wisdom to tell the future.

The Word of Knowledge

The second gift in the category of revelation is the word of knowledge. We could add an extra word and call it a gift of the word of *God's* knowledge. Then there would be no mistaking it for man's knowledge.

The word "knowledge" is related to fact. If a thing is knowledge, then it is not mystery. The gift of the word of knowledge deals with that which exists, whether it be in the past or in the present. In the gift of the word of knowledge God reveals to one of His servants something which now exists or did exist on the earth. This must be something which that servant could not know naturally — something his eyes have not seen and his ears have not heard. Normally it would have to do with the meeting of an emergency. God would not reveal such a thing if there was no real purpose for doing so.

Word of Knowledge in the Old Testament

Here are some examples of the gift of the word of knowledge operating in the Old Testament:

Elijah

In 1 Kings, chapter 19, Elijah is speaking. Beginning in verse 14, he says:

I have been very jealous for the Lord God of hosts: because the children of Israel have forsaken thy covenant, thrown down thine altars, and slain thy prophets with the sword; and I, even I only, am left; and they seek my life, to take it away.

I would say that Elijah was a little discouraged. He thought he was the only one left. Have you ever thought you were the only one left? That's just how Elijah felt.

And the Lord said unto him, Go, return on thy way to the wilderness of Damascus: and when thou comest, anoint Hazael to be king over Syria:

And Jehu the son of Nimshi shalt thou anoint to be king over Israel: and Elisha the son of Shaphat of Abel-meholah shalt thou anoint to be prophet in thy room.

And it shall come to pass, that him that escapeth the sword of Hazael shall Jehu slay: and him that escapeth from the sword of Jehu shall Elisha slay.

Now notice verse 18:

Yet I have left me seven thousand in Israel, all the knees which have not bowed unto Baal, and every mouth which hath not kissed him.

So here we find a prophet named Elijah, who of his own knowledge says, "You know, there is not another good man living except me." This is a strong statement to make, especially when you are talking to God. Elijah says, "All the preachers are gone. I'm the only preacher left."

But then God revealed to Elijah a word of knowledge. God said to him: "You said there wasn't one except you. I'm now revealing to you that there are 7,000 more, and not one of them has bowed his knee to Baal, not one of them has reached over and kissed this idol. Everyone of them is free from idol worship. Why don't you just do what I tell you to do? Get busy. Go and anoint Jehu as king and Elisha as prophet."

There have been times when I have spent so much time answering letters and dealing with problems, that I began to feel as if I were part of the problem. So I just stood up, walked out of my office, got in my car, drove to the hospital, and began to pray for people. I stepped out from behind my desk and got out there where the needs were. Instantly, something was revived inside me. I felt brand new!

Elijah had been out of connection. He had been out on his own and did not realize that God had an army. God revealed through a word of His knowledge that at that moment there were 7,000 men in Israel who had not bowed their knees to Baal. They had stood up straight, refusing to have any part in idol worship. They were God's wonderful servants for that hour, and He knew their names, their addresses, and their abilities.

Elijah knew nothing about it, so God had to reveal it to him supernaturally. That is what is meant by a word of God's knowledge. God reveals something that you do not know naturally.

Elisha

A very remarkable incident is found in 2 Kings 5:20-27. It is the story of Elisha and Gehazi. Elisha had succeeded the prophet Elijah who had gone on to heaven.

Naaman, a very wealthy Syrian general, had come to Elisha and received a remarkable healing from leprosy. After being healed, Naaman turned to the prophet and said, "I want to give you a gift."

But Elisha said, "I don't want any gifts. You are healed. Just thank God for it and go on home." Naaman had already promised to quit worshiping idols.

Gehazi, Elisha's servant, decided to take the offering that Elisha turned down, so he ran after Naaman's chariot. When Naaman stopped, Gehazi said to him, "Since you were there, two men have come from a great distance and they need some money and some clothes." So Naaman gave him what he asked for. When Gehazi took the offering, he had no intention of telling the prophet.

When Gehazi returned home, Elisha spoke to him and said, "Did not my spirit go right along with you? Did not I see the whole thing that happened?" The gift of the word of God's knowledge was operating through Elisha. He watched in the spirit realm as Gehazi took the money from Naaman.

This man Elisha had a most remarkable manifestation of this gift. The word of knowledge functioned more times through him than anyone else in the Old Testament.

In 2 Kings, chapter 6, when the alien armies of Syria were coming against his country, Elisha sent word to his king and said, "They are at the southeast corner tonight, and they are hiding. Just go get them." So the king went out and won the battle.

A few days later, Elisha said, "They have come back again. They are on that northwest corner in hiding. They are behind those certain bushes and trees. Go get them."

Finally the Syrian king said, "Somebody among us is a spy and is telling the king of Israel where our army is."

They said, "No, no, King, there is no spy among us. We are all true. They've got a prophet among them named Elisha, and he knows everything. He knows where we are and what we are doing."

Again, we see the functioning of the word of God's knowledge. God made Elisha to know where those armies were, so that he could communicate it to his king.

Samuel

In 1 Samuel, chapter 10, we find a very interesting example. The prophet Samuel wanted Saul to become king of the country of Israel. The people of Israel were going to have a great celebration and inauguration of Saul as king over their country; but Saul was reticent. He did not want to be part of it. Though Saul was a big man, standing head and shoulders above anyone else in the land, he hid himself in a haystack on the day of the inauguration.

Nobody could find him until the prophet Samuel arrived. Samuel prayed to the Lord, and the Lord gave him the answer. Samuel received a word of God's knowledge. He knew that which his eyes had not seen and his ears had not heard. God through the Holy Spirit told Samuel exactly where Saul was. Samuel said, *Behold, he hath hid himself among the stuff* (v. 22). The people then found Saul and made him king.

This gift was manifested in other instances as well. One time when Saul had lost some asses, Samuel said, "I can tell you where they are." And he did.

In the Old Testament we have some very vivid operations of the omniscience of God, how He revealed certain things through a word of His knowledge and showed the people how they could supernaturally understand the knowledge He had.

Other Old Testament examples can be found. In 2 Kings 6:12 the king's servant said of Elisha, . . . *the prophet that is in Israel, telleth the king of Israel the words that thou speakest in thy bedchamber.*

I suggest that you research and study these Old Testament stories until you become conversant in them. Then find other examples where God revealed His knowledge supernaturally to the people.

Word of Knowledge in the New Testament

In the New Testament our Lord Jesus exercised this gift, and He exercised it with divine authority.

In John's Gospel, chapter 4, we see the story of Jesus and the woman at the well. Jesus came to a well in Sychar, a town north of Jerusalem. As He was sitting there by the well at about the sixth hour (about noon), a woman came to draw water. This was most unusual because that was not the normal time people drew water. At noon the sun is hot and the jug heavy, so they usually drew water early in the morning or in the evening.

At noon Jesus was seated by the well, no doubt thirsty, when the woman walked up. He said to her, "Would you give me a drink of water, please?" It was a deep well, and He needed her to use her rope to lower her jar into the water.

She looked at Him and said, "You are a Jew; I'm a Samaritan. We don't have any fellowship. What do you mean asking me for water? We don't get along at all."

Then Jesus rebuffed her by saying, "If you would have asked of Me, I would have given you living water and you would never have thirsted again."

Immediately she said, "Do you mean you are greater than our father Jacob who dug this well and that you have water that would keep me from ever being thirsty again? Give me some of this water."

Then Jesus said, "Call your husband."

"I'm not married."

He said, "You told the truth then. You've had five husbands already, and the fellow you are living with now isn't your husband."

She got so excited that she left her jug and went running back into the city. She said to the men,

"Come and see a man who told me everything I have done!"

Here we have the functioning of the word of God's knowledge. Jesus knew fact after fact after fact. When He revealed these facts to that Samaritan woman, she was startled. When she came back and told the people, the whole city received a surge of God.

I have found that if you will permit the gifts of the Spirit to function, you will have a movement of souls that will come to you like never before. When the gifts function, souls are saved every time. Just let the gifts of the Spirit begin to function and people will pour into the Kingdom of God!

Peter and Cornelius

In the Acts of the Apostles, chapter 10, we see the story of Peter and a vision he received while at Joppa. After he saw the vision and was thinking about it, the Spirit of God spoke to him and said, Behold, three men seek thee (v. 19).

These men were sent by a man named Cornelius who was at Caesarea. Caesarea is a town located on the coast a number of miles north of Joppa. Peter was in Joppa and Cornelius was in Caesarea. The Bible says that as Cornelius was praying, the Lord spoke to him and said, "In Joppa, at the house of Simon the tanner, is a fellow named Peter. Tell him to come up here, and he'll give you the words of truth."

That was a word of God's knowledge. God supernaturally gave Cornelius knowledge of Peter's whereabouts. So Cornelius sent three men south to Joppa to find Peter. When these three messengers came to inquire at the house of Simon the tanner, we find that God had already spoken to Peter and given him the word of knowledge, saying, "Standing down at the gate are three men, and I want you to go with them." Peter knew supernaturally by a word of God's knowledge that these men were at the gate.

So here we see from the New Testament how a word of God's knowledge functioned through His people. Peter and Cornelius knew facts they could never have known otherwise. Because of it in this instance, the whole Gentile world was opened to the Gospel of Jesus Christ. These were the first Gentiles to move in the word of knowledge from God.

Word of Knowledge in Operation

A few years ago while I was conducting a revival meeting in Tulsa, Oklahoma, a lady invited me to dinner. After dinner, she had me sit in a rocking chair; then she looked at me and said, "Brother Sumrall, some of the people at our church think I'm a witch." She then related the following story to me:

One morning as she was sitting in that rocking chair, reading her Bible, the thought came to her that her son, daughter-in-law, and grandchildren were going fishing. She saw them hitch the boat trailer to their car, drive to a lake about fifty miles outside of Tulsa, and park under a tree at the end of the lake. She saw them back up the car, put the trailer into the water, release the boat, put all their fishing gear into the boat, and push away from shore. Then she saw her son reach over to one of the children and cause the boat to capsize. Immediately, she knew that all five of them had drowned.

Nothing like that had ever happened to her before. She grabbed the phone and dialed her son's number, but there was no answer. Then she called the fire department and told them the story. At first they thought she was crazy, but because of her persistence, they agreed to check out her story. They went to the lake and found the place she described. A car was parked there with a boat trailer in the water, and away from shore a boat was floating upside down. After dragging that area of the lake, the firemen recovered the five bodies.

She said, "Brother Sumrall, am I a witch?"

I said, "No, you had one of the gifts of the Spirit functioning in you. God showed you through the word of knowledge exactly where they were and what had happened. Otherwise, they might have been there for a long time before anybody found them."

You may ask, "Why didn't God stop it?" I cannot say. I have no idea if they were saved and if they had any relationship with God at all. I only know that as a godly, Spirit-filled mother was reading her Bible, God opened her spirit and gave her the gift of the word of knowledge.

The Discerning of Spirits

The third gift of revelation is the discerning of spirits.

What It Is Not

The discerning of spirits has no relationship to that which is natural. It is not some kind of metaphysical operation. It is not thought reading. It is not psychoanalysis or projection of extrasensory perception. It has nothing to do with the realm of the mind. Some people claim to have "the gift of discernment," but there is no such gift. It is not a discernment of things; it is the discernment of spirits.

There are three areas in which this gift can operate: the divine, the demonic, and the human or natural. I must emphatically state that this gift is not primarily a discerning of devils, though some people hold that view. It is divinely comprehending and understanding a human spirit — the kind of spirit a person possesses.

This gift is not a clash of human personalities. Sometimes when a wife has had a fight with her husband, she may think he is possessed of the devil.

The discerning of spirits certainly is not the gift of suspicion — suspecting a person of being a certain way when he is not that way at all.

What It Is and What It Does

The discerning of spirits is the divine ability to see the presence and activity of a spirit that motivates a human being, whether good or bad. This revelation comes to the Church through the functioning of the Holy Ghost.

The discerning of spirits gives members of the Body of Christ insight into the spirit world, a realm which their five physical senses — feeling, hearing, seeing, smelling, tasting — cannot enter. The telescope can reveal the amazing stars in space. The microscope can bring to light the intricate mysteries of microscopic life. But it takes the gift of discerning of spirits to penetrate to the dividing of soul and spirit within a person.

This discerning of spirits can bring tremendous inspiration to a church body. It can produce a real spirit of security against false doctrines, lies, and all kinds of things that are unreal. It can enable a church to choose the proper men and women to fulfil their ministries within the church.

Bible Examples of Discerning of Spirits

Let's look into the Word of God and see some of the remarkable instances of discerning of spirits.

Simon, the Soothsayer

In Acts, chapter 8, a man named Simon looked on with wonder as Peter and John laid their hands on people to receive the gift of the Holy Ghost.

This man, who was a soothsayer, thought in his heart: "If only I had such power. It would make me a big man among the people. Every man has a price; I'll persuade these men to sell this power to me." So he went to the apostles and said, "I'd like to give you money for that power." (vv. 18,19.)

Peter looked at him and said:

Thy money perish with thee, because thou hast thought that the gift of God may be purchased with money.

Thou hast neither part nor lot in this matter: for thy heart is not right in the sight of God.

Repent therefore of this thy wickedness, and pray God, if perhaps the thought of thine heart may be forgiven thee.

For I perceive that thou art in the gall of bitterness, and in the bond of iniquity.

Acts 8:20-23

Here was a man in the church fellowship who, when he saw this supernatural manifestation, said: "I'm going to grab that. I'm going to buy it and use it and make money with it."

Until it was revealed by the Holy Ghost, the others did not understand. But Peter was seeing something that could not be seen with the physical eye and he said, "You are in the gall of bitterness, the bond of iniquity." We cannot make merchandise out of the works of God.

Dozens of times people have come to me for prayer and tried to leave money. I say to them: "If you want to give money, go to church and give it. Don't give it to me when I have prayed a prayer of faith for your deliverance. You can't pay for the blessings of God."

Elymas, the Sorcerer

In Acts 13:6-12 we find Paul discerning the evil tendencies of Elymas, the sorcerer:

Then Saul, (who also is called Paul,) filled with the Holy Ghost, set his eyes on him, and said, O full of all subtilty and all mischief, thou child of the devil, thou enemy of all righteousness, wilt thou not cease to pervert the right ways of the Lord? (vv. 9,10).

Elymas may have looked as normal and natural as anybody, but Paul by the discerning of spirits looked straight through him and told his whole life story.

Ananias and Sapphira

In the Acts of the Apostles, chapter 5, we read about a certain couple in the Church, Ananias and Sapphira. In their church fellowship there was a man who became very popular. The apostles named him Barnabas, which means "the son of consolation." He got that name by selling all his property and giving the money to the Church.

Ananias and Sapphira decided they, too, wanted to be popular in the Church, so they sold their property. But when they held that big bag of money, they thought: "This is too much to give the Church. Let's keep back part of it. No one will ever know." (But the Bible says in Numbers 32:23, *Be sure your sin will find you out.*)

Ananias wanted to take the money down to the church right then, so he got his bag of money and went running down to the church. The people said, "Here comes Ananias. Look at the big bag of money he has. He sold his property and is going to give it all to the Church!"

When Ananias stood before Peter with his bag of gold, he said, "Peter, you know how Barnabas sold his property there in Cyprus and became such a wonderful person in the Church? We sold our property, too, so we're going to give all of our money to the Church!"

Peter looked at him and said, "All of it?"

"Oh, yes, all of it."

Peter was a good ball player; he wanted to give Ananias three strikes before calling him out. He said, "Now, Ananias, you are speaking before the Body and you are speaking before God. Is this all of it?"

"All of it." Strike one!

"Ananias, that is a large bag of money. It must have been beautiful property. Is all of it in there?"

"It's all in there." Strike two!

"Ananias, did God tell you to sell your property and give the money to the Church?"

"Yes, God told me to. All of the money is in the bag." Strike three — you're out! Ananias dropped

79

dead right there in church! Some young men in the church took up his body and buried it.

About three hours later Sapphira walked in, expecting to get a lot of praise that day. After all, they had given a bag of gold to the Church! When she saw Peter, she said, "Oh, Peter, aren't you proud of us? We sold our property and gave all the money to the Church."

"All?"

"Yes, sir. Hasn't Ananias told you about it?"

He said, "Sapphira, do you know how much you sold it for?"

"Yes. It was all in that bag."

"Sapphira, I'm going to ask you one more time: When your husband left the house to come down here to the church, was all the money in that bag?"

"Oh, yes!" She fell down dead!

When Peter saw Ananias, the gift of discerning of spirits came into manifestation. Peter knew immediately that Ananias was lying to God, and Ananias paid the price for it!

Discerning of Spirits at Work Today

A number of years ago, I was present in a small Wednesday-night prayer meeting. A beautiful young woman, a stranger, came into the auditorium and sat toward the back. When there was a pause in the meeting, she stood up and said, "I'm an evangelist, and God has told me to conduct a special revival campaign in this church. No one is to resist me because I am God's servant and the revival must begin tonight. The Lord has sent me here to bless you and to preach to you."

Her words brought a strange coldness over the meeting. There was a moment of quietness. To one side of the auditorium sat a little lady with head bowed. Suddenly, she stood to her feet and, with her face raised to heaven, said, "You are a harlot from St. Louis, Missouri. (The woman had said she was from another city.) You are in this town living with a man to whom you are not married. You have boasted to him that you could come to this church, deceive these people, preach to them, and collect an offering without their knowing you are a harlot. If you do not repent, you will die before you leave this building."

God's power fell heavily on the church and all of us fell to our knees in prayer. When we lifted our heads, the woman was gone. The discerning of spirits had revealed the truth and she fled from it.

My Experience in Java

In Java as I was walking down the church aisle, a woman caught me by my sleeve. When I turned to see what she wanted, she said, "You have a black angel in you, and I have a white angel in me."

As I turned around, God spoke through my lips and said, "I have a white angel in me, not black; but you *do* have a black angel in you; and I command you now to come out of her!"

The woman was set free at that moment. Her eyes, which had been glassy, were instantly made clear. Her face changed its appearance. She had been under the power of that demonic spirit for fifteen years!

Through the discerning of spirits, I immediately knew that there was a foul spirit within her, a spirit of evil. That was knowledge I would not have received any other way. She looked as normal as the other people in that congregation. Had you asked me to walk among them and pick out such a person, I would not have been able to do it. God had to reveal it to me. When the spirit within her moved, I was able to identify it and cast it out in Jesus' name through the gift of the Spirit that operated in me.

A Gift to Cleanse the Churches

The gift of discerning of spirits is an excellent instrument to clean out the pulpits and pews of America. Many pastors and church leaders today are engaged in activities that are not right and honest and true. Church members as well are living in sin, doing things totally opposed to the will of God for their lives. Through the discerning of spirits, we can have a holy Church without spot or wrinkle.

But are we willing for this gift of the Spirit to function? That is the place we must reach, where we are ready and willing for the gifts of the Spirit to function in their fullness among us.

The discerning of spirits is a gift which enables one to appraise motives. But more than this, it gives the believer power to see what others do not see. As Howard Carter has stated: "The discerning of spirits is a gift of the Holy Spirit by which the possessor is enabled to see into the spirit world. By this insight he can discern the similitude of God, the risen Christ, the Holy Spirit, cherubim and seraphim, the archangels and the host of angels, or Satan and his legions."

8
The Power Gifts

The second category of spiritual gifts is actually an artillery of gifts known as the gifts of power: the gift of faith, the gifts of healing, and the working of miracles. These gifts are second in appreciation and second in greatness, the revelation gifts being the greatest God can give.

The Gift of Faith

We must recognize, first of all, that there are many kinds of faith. Sometimes the gift of faith is mistaken for the simple faith it takes for salvation. But the two are not the same.

Everyone has faith, the Bible says so: *God hath dealt to every man the measure of faith* (Rom. 12:3). This type of universal faith has no relation to the supernatural sign gift of the Holy Spirit we are studying about here. There is a difference between the measure of faith, which the Bible says is given to every believer, and the gift of faith.

Natural Faith

There is a natural faith which human beings have — the kind of faith a farmer has when he sows seed. He plants a seed of corn, believing that it will die, burst open, come up out of the ground as a simple little blade, and grow into a healthy stalk that will produce more corn. The farmer has faith for that; otherwise, rather than planting the corn seed, he would eat it. That is an example of natural faith.

A fisherman has this same kind of natural faith. He believes that if he goes out on a lake and casts his net in the right spot at the right time in the right way, he will catch fish. And he is generally successful in his belief.

Saving Faith

In the spiritual realm there is a kind of faith we call "saving faith." A person hears the Gospel of Jesus Christ, believes it, accepts Jesus into his heart, and is saved. That is saving faith.

Every redeemed person in the world has this saving faith, but not every person has the gift of faith. The thief on the cross next to Jesus had saving faith. (Luke 23:42,43.) He just believed on Jesus and received his salvation as he hung there on that cross. He had no time to receive the gift of faith from the Spirit.

The Philippian jailer had saving faith. He fell at the feet of Paul and Silas and asked, *Sirs, what must I do to be saved?* They responded, *Believe on the Lord Jesus Christ, and thou shalt be saved* (Acts 16:30,31). He believed and was converted.

We need this kind of faith to become converted and we need it to receive healing. We say, "Lord, I bring my disease to You. I believe that by Your stripes I am healed. I accept it, thank You for it, and confess that I've got it now."

The Gift of Faith Is Special

The gift of faith is different from other types of faith. It is a special faith that supernaturally achieves what is impossible through human instruments. We observe the gift of faith in operation when God, through the power of the Holy Spirit, performs supernatural exploits that cannot be humanly explained. These exploits cannot be what is done ordinarily; otherwise, they would have no relation to the supernatural gifts of the Holy Spirit.

This kind of miracle has to be something which a human being could not do normally. There is no human strength involved in it. This fact must be clearly understood: The gift of faith has to do with the functioning of God in you and through you, but with no human strength involved on your part. You do nothing. In this gift, God does something supernaturally on your behalf.

The gift of faith can operate in areas of divine protection and divine provision. But in whatever area it works, it works independent of you. You do nothing about it; God does it all for you. It is the power of faith functioning gloriously and amazingly in your behalf, just as it functioned through Jesus. He spoke mighty words to the tempest, and immediately it was calmed. That was faith functioning through Him. He did nothing but speak words of faith, and it was done.

Most Christians probably do not believe they drink from the same fountain Jesus drank from, but they do. We have the same kind of power flowing through us that flowed through Jesus.

This truth came dramatically to me. I was not taught as a boy that we could be anything like Jesus. I thought men like Moses and the Apostle Paul had a special inroad with God that I would never be able to experience. It was exciting when I discovered that I was a participator in the same strength, the same power, the same vitality, the same wisdom, and the same knowledge that Jesus had.

Unlimited Faith

The gift of faith has been manifested by many of God's servants. It is evidenced when a supernatural event occurs with no human effort.

Faith permits God to perform in your behalf. This gift of faith is unlimited for the simple reason that God, not man, is the door. God is the source of its energy. If this were not the case, then the gift of faith would have to be limited as are some of the other spiritual gifts. (The gifts of healing is a limited gift, as we will discover later.)

The gift of faith deals with "more than conquerors." (Rom. 8:37.) A conqueror is a person who meets another person of equal strength and knocks him out. A person who is more than a conqueror just stands and says, "Fall," and down goes that other person!

The gift of faith functions in all those who are more than conquerors. God does something while your hands are closed. That means you are more than a conqueror. He does the fighting; you do the rejoicing! In the gift of faith God does all the work. I do not mean to imply that you are lazy. You simply have the anointing and the power of God within you. You speak it, and God does it.

If you say, "It can't be done," you are right — it can't, in your life. You cannot function in God without faith. That is why you should read the Bible every day. *Faith cometh by hearing, and hearing by the word of God* (Rom. 10:17).

86

The Gift of Faith Illustrated

The gift of faith functions on behalf of the believer to bring about that which otherwise would not be possible through that person's efforts.

Let's illustrate this gift of faith with some examples from the Word of God.

Moses

Moses, according to the Word of God, took his staff and dropped it at the feet of the greatest king of his day, Pharaoh of Egypt. Pharaoh was the strongest monarch upon the face of the earth at that time. His was *the* kingdom of strength on earth.

When Moses laid down his shepherd's staff, it suddenly changed into a king cobra. So Pharaoh called in his magicians. When they threw down their staffs, they, too, became serpents — but Moses' serpent devoured theirs! When Moses reached down and took up the cobra, it became a staff again. (Ex. 7:10-13.)

Here was a functioning of sovereign power in Moses' behalf. Moses had nothing to do with what happened. He was just an observer of what God did, and it was a miracle, very convincing to the monarch. Pharaoh finally let the children of Israel leave the land of Egypt because of the mighty miraculous signs that Moses called into being. Moses called the miracles into being and God performed them. The great power of God was demonstrated without Moses even lifting a finger; he just folded his hands.

Elijah

This gift of faith is beautifully shown to us in the life of Elijah, God's prophet. In 1 Kings, chapter 17,

87

Elijah was hidden away in the wilderness with nothing to eat (and there were no bakeries or shops close by!). The Lord caused the ravens to bring meat and bread to Elijah. It was a miracle that the ravens did not eat the food before it reached Elijah, because that is their natural way of doing things. But God is able to take that which ordinarily happens and change it to suit His purposes.

Elijah did nothing to get his meals. There was no labor on his part, none whatsoever. He just said, "Lord, I thank You for supplying my needs."

Here we find that, not only did God supply Elijah his bread and meat there, but when the brook dried up, God told Elijah: *Arise, get thee to Zarephath . . . behold, I have commanded a widow woman there to sustain thee* (1 Kings 17:9). When Elijah reached Zarephath, he found that the widow also was about to die.

He asked her for some bread and water, and she told him: *I have not a cake, but an handful of meal in a barrel, and a little oil in a cruse: and, behold, I am gathering two sticks, that I may go in and dress it for me and my son, that we may eat it, and die* (v. 12).

In response, Elijah spoke words of faith and comfort to her. He said: *Fear not; go and do as thou hast said: but make me thereof a little cake first, and bring it unto me, and after make for thee and for thy son* (v. 13).

Elijah told her to make him a little cake first. You know, when we pay our tithes to God *first*, we are going to get first treatment from Him. God will

88

treat us that way, and I want first-class treatment from God, don't you?

So the woman prepared the cake and gave it to Elijah first, and through the command of this prophet of God, *she, and he, and her house, did eat many days. And the barrel of meal wasted not, neither did the cruse of oil fail, according to the word of the Lord which he spake by Elijah* (vv. 15,16). The woman was supernaturally fed through three years of famine because of the word spoken by God's man, Elijah. That was a gift of faith to Elijah.

Elisha

Another example of the gift of faith in operation is in 2 Kings, chapter 6. Elisha had his Bible school boys out cutting down some trees. When one of the students hit a tree with an ax, the ax head flew off and fell into the Jordan River. . . . *and he cried, and said, Alas, master! for it was borrowed. And the man of God said, Where fell it? And he shewed him the place. And he cut down a stick, and cast it in thither; and the iron did swim* (vv. 5,6).

The man of God, Elisha, acted in the gift of faith, illustrating the power of that gift.

Seven of the nine gifts of the Spirit functioned in the Old Testament. (The only two of the nine gifts that began with the New Testament are tongues and the interpretation of tongues.) These seven gifts in the Old Testament did not function in the same way as in the New Testament. They came upon men only at special times in special situations.

Elisha was one of the most remarkable of these men. Read 2 Kings, chapters 2-13, and notice how many times Elisha demonstrated the word of knowledge. He functioned in the word of knowledge more than anyone of his day. Read beginning with the time Elijah called him into service until his death and see how many times he supernaturally understood things from a distance. It is a very enlightening study.

Daniel

Daniel was a remarkable man of faith. Having been brought from his homeland of Israel into Babylon, he was a refugee; but more than that, Daniel was a prisoner of war. He was such a handsome, clever fellow that he was put into training with the other young men. He was so clever, in fact, that he soon rose to the top and, with some of his friends, was actually ruling Babylon.

The Babylonians became jealous of Daniel because of his remarkable wisdom, which was actually coming from God. He had a Source of information, a Source of blessing, which the Babylonians knew nothing about.

Out of jealousy, these men spied on Daniel to find something for which they could accuse him before the king. When they found him praying three times a day to Jehovah, they managed to trick the king into passing a law, proclaiming that prayer could be offered to no one except the king of Babylon. They made their king into a god, not because they loved him, but because they hated Daniel. The penalty for anyone disobeying this law was to be thrown into a special den of lions.

Daniel knew about the law, but his faith was so strong that he would not stop praying to his God. He prayed with his windows wide open for all to hear and see. Eventually he was arrested and brought before the king. When the king realized what had happened, he was very sorry about the situation, but had no choice except to condemn Daniel and command that he be cast into the den of lions.

The king must have had faith in Daniel's faith, though, because he told him: *Thy God whom thou servest continually, he will deliver thee* (Dan. 6:16). And the next morning he hurried to check on Daniel. He must have had faith or he would not have done that. He simply would have sent out servants to pick up Daniel's bones. When he reached the den, he found Daniel safe and sound, ready to go back to work. How did that happen? By the power of faith!

When Daniel was placed in the den of lions, he was immediately the master of the situation. He did not hurt the beasts; he did not ask God for power to tear them to pieces. He simply radiated a force which caused the lions to lie down in perfect peace as he slept among them. Daniel personally did nothing; it was God Who performed the amazing miracle. The gift of faith was in action!

Daniel told the king: *My God hath sent his angel, and hath shut the lions' mouths, that they have not hurt me* (v. 22).

The Three Hebrew Children

As we see in Daniel's case, the gift of faith is the opposite of fear. There is no sense of fear or apprehension or uncertainty involved in faith. If there is, then it is not faith. Faith only functions in serenity, confidence, and peace.

One of the choicest illustrations of this faith action, I believe, is that of the three Hebrew children in the Book of Daniel, chapter 3. These three young men — Shadrach, Meshach, and Abednego — refused to bow down and worship the golden image of Nebuchadnezzar, the king of Babylon. When Nebuchadnezzar heard of this, he commanded that they be placed in a fiery furnace that had been heated seven times hotter than usual. (Dan. 3:19,20.)

When they were cast into the furnace, Shadrach, Meshach, and Abednego made no effort to fight the flames. They did not resist, nor did they complain.

When the king looked in, he said in shock, *Did not we cast three men bound into the midst of the fire?* (v. 24).

His men answered, "Yes."

He answered and said, Lo, I see four men loose, walking in the midst of the fire, and they have no hurt; and the form of the fourth is like the Son of God (v. 25).

And it was! Jesus was walking among them. When those three Hebrew children walked out of that furnace, not a hair of their heads was singed and not even the smell of fire was about them! (v. 27.)

Here we find in operation the dynamic gift of faith. These men, thrown into a furnace, had no way to exercise their own strength or power. Yet they walked out of that furnace without having resisted or fought it in any way. That is faith! It was the gift of faith, a supernatural faith, an instance in which supernatural things take place because people believe.

If those men had not believed, they would have died in that fire. If they had been fearful, they would have died. But they stepped into the furnace with courage and with honor, and they came marching out unscathed! They had an element with them called faith and it functioned in their total being. That is the gift of faith.

The Gift of Faith in My Life

I entered into the ministry with a kind of faith that perhaps many young men of my time did not possess. The day I walked out the front door of my father's house to become a preacher, I had just a few coins in my pocket, but I was not concerned. I knew only one thing: I was called of God to preach the Gospel of the Lord Jesus Christ.

Many people would never enter into full-time ministry with no resources at all; but to me it seemed the only thing to do, and I had no problem doing it. I had no negative thought about it; I just did it.

Three years later, I was in San Francisco, ready to set out around the world as a missionary. For three nights before boarding the ship, I preached in a very large church for which I received no offering. I had to look to God as my Source.

When the pastor of that church took me to the boat, he proceeded to tell me how I would starve to death in China. In response, I said that if I did, I wanted him to send a little tombstone to China which read: "Here lies Lester Sumrall, who starved to death trusting Jesus."

He said, "I won't do it!"

I said, "I won't need it!"

Those were my last words on mainland America. I boarded ship and sailed away, headed for

Australia and New Zealand to start preaching around the world.

Throughout my journey, God provided for me locally. I had no contacts in America, no churches contributing to my support. God supernaturally provided for my every need. I lived in a constant state of having to believe God for my next day's transportation. Sometimes when traveling long distances, such as across Siberia and Russia, we had to pay in advance. I always had the necessary money at the proper time.

For our trip to Tibet, which took three months on muleback, we had to hire a cook, an interpreter, and 17 pack animals. A few nights before we were to leave, I had no funds to pay for the trip. The Lord provided the whole amount through one Chinese woman, a general's wife, to whom I had ministered healing from our Lord Jesus.

In the function and operation of faith, you do not scream and cry, "What am I going to do?" You must rely on God to meet your need. We just rejoiced in the Lord, and it came to pass!

The Gift of Faith in Smith Wigglesworth

I was very well acquainted with Smith Wigglesworth, having visited in his home many times before he passed away. He was certainly a dynamic man of faith.

Smith Wigglesworth and his wife met and were married in the Salvation Army. Though a plumber by trade, he worked with his wife in a local mission. He was slow of speech, so he handed out songbooks and took up the offering, while his wife did the preaching.

But there was something big inside Smith Wigglesworth. When he prayed for people, things happened. He demonstrated some amazing feats of faith in his life.

One day, when he came home from work, he was met at the door with news that his wife had died — that she had been dead for two hours.

To that, Wigglesworth replied, "No, she's not dead." He dropped his lunch bucket and tools, walked into the bedroom, pulled her out of bed, stood her against the wall, called her by her first name, and said, "I command you to come to me now!" Then he backed off, and here she came! She lived a number of years after that.

Faith was a primary strength in the life and ministry of Smith Wigglesworth. He knew what it was to have the gift of faith.

The Gift of Faith in Howard Carter

Many beautiful operations of this special gift of faith occurred in the life of Howard Carter.

At one time, Rev. Carter made arrangements to purchase by faith a church for a local congregation in London, England. He was given 60 days to pay the note. At the time he was president of Hampstead Bible School. As the days and weeks went by and no money came in, the faculty and students became very concerned. They were so nervous in fact that the last day or two they found it difficult to eat — everyone, that is, except Rev. Carter. His appetite was as good as usual.

The night before the day of foreclosure on the property, there still were no funds; but Rev. Carter was a man of faith. He said very simply, "God has assured me that I will have the full payment on schedule. I don't have the money now, but I don't need it until tomorrow."

The last mail delivery in London is 9:00 P.M. As Rev. Carter picked up the mail from the box, there was a large brown envelope. As he himself told me: "I picked up the envelope and laid it on the mantle with the other mail. I was going to leave it there until the next morning. Usually when I get a large brown package like that, it is a load of clippings that someone has sent for me to read."

But the Lord spoke to his heart and said, "Open it tonight."

He argued for a while, but finally surrendered to that urging within his spirit. When he tore open the package, he found a bundle of new pound notes from the bank — exactly the amount he needed to purchase the church.

There was no name or return address on the envelope. The gift was anonymous. God oftentimes provides for His servants that way.

Anyone else would have jumped up and down, shouted with excitement, and run upstairs to tell everybody what had happened. Not Rev. Carter. He very calmly placed the envelope on the shelf where it had been and went to bed.

The next morning at breakfast, he told the students and faculty about their blessing. Then he passed around the brown envelope for all to see. While everybody went wild with joy and excitement, Rev. Carter hardly wrinkled his face. He said, "I knew it two months ago and I was sure of it two months ago. I told the Lord I wasn't nervous about when He would send it. I didn't need it until 11 A.M. that certain day, so any time before that would be fine."

Another great demonstration of the gift of faith occurred when Rev. Carter was in prison during World War I, serving time as a conscientious objector. He was placed in a cell so narrow that he could not move around. The concrete roof above him leaked, and the dripping of water on his head was extremely aggravating.

Finally, one night he said, "Lord, stop that leak."

The Lord answered, "No, I won't stop it. You stop it."

"But, Lord, how can I stop it?"

"Speak to it."

That is when Howard Carter discovered his power with God. Lying on a cot in a prison cell, iron bars on each side, a concrete roof above him, water peppering down on his head, Rev. Carter spoke to the water. He commanded it to flow the other way. At that moment, the leak stopped and not another drop of water came through during the war! It was a dynamic act of the gift of faith.

Howard Carter was a man of solid truth. I lived with him for many years and never knew him to exaggerate. Whatever he told was absolute truth.

The Gifts of Healing

The gifts of healing may possibly be the most controversial of the nine gifts of the Spirit. It is the only gift of the nine that is in the plural form, the only gift that has to do with more than one aspect, which would lead to the question: How many gifts of healing are there?

It has been suggested that there are possibly as many categories of disease in the world as there were stripes placed upon Jesus' back. He received 39 stripes and, according to Isaiah 53:5, *with his stripes we are healed.*

Jesus was very careful to differentiate between the various kinds of sicknesses and diseases He came up against. For example, in Matthew 17 He dealt with a little boy who would throw himself into the fire and into the water. Of this, He said, *Howbeit this kind goeth not out but by prayer and fasting* (v. 21). The Lord was showing that special attention had to be given to someone who is being relieved of satanic oppressions — that there had to be special preparation — a cleansing of the one who was to deliver the healing.

A Limited Gift

Why is "the gifts of healing" the only gift that is actually limited? Why cannot one minister have all nine gifts of the Spirit?

The Lord Jesus is the only person who possessed consistent, perfect gifts of healing in His ministry. He never failed to heal. The Apostle Paul could not heal everyone. He even left behind a certain member of his own evangelistic party for the simple reason, the Bible says, that he was sick. (2 Tim. 4:20.) Even Simon Peter had to call upon Jesus to heal his mother-in-law. (Matt. 8:14.)

There is a divine purpose for this: If all nine gifts of the Spirit functioned through one channel, that person would then be like God. If he healed all people that were sick whenever he wanted to, he would be accepted by the world as God. If one human being had the ability to heal every disease among men, he would be unable to withstand the praise, honor, and riches that would be lavished upon him. I have seen it happen in the last forty years, both in England and in America.

Here are some examples of healing ministries that have risen during the twentieth century:

Alexander Dowie

Probably no ministry in modern times had more amazing miracles of healing than that of Dr. John Alexander Dowie. With Chicago as his home base, Dowie developed a ministry in the power of God that brought him worldwide fame. In 1900, he purchased a 6,000-acre tract of land north of Chicago where he built the city of Zion. Within two years this new city had grown to a population of 10,000.

The public acclaim and adoration that Dowie received was more than he could withstand. As the result of "divine revelations," he began to see himself as "Elijah the prophet" and the "first apostle" of the Church. His personal proclamations, plus financial irresponsibility, caused Dowie's followers to revolt against his tyrannical control.

Though he experienced tremendous miracles of healing during the years of his ministry, Alexander Dowie died a broken man in 1907.

Stephen Jeffreys

Another great healing minister was Stephen Jeffreys, a Welshman. Through Jeffreys' ministry, hundreds of people were healed of various ailments; but there was a particular anointing in his life for the healing of rheumatoid arthritis. Howard Carter said that in Brother Jeffreys' great crusades in England, some people in wheelchairs were so crippled with rheumatoid arthritis that their faces could not be seen.

One night during a crusade, Brother Jeffreys started laughing in the spirit. Then he jumped off the platform, went over to a man, and lifted him from the wheelchair. Within three minutes, that man was running up and down the aisles, pushing his wheelchair! Without a doubt, the gifts of healing operated in Jeffreys' ministry.

When the sick are healed, people want to lavish gifts upon the minister who was God's instrument in their healing. As a result, Stephen Jeffreys became a wealthy man. According to Howard Carter, Jeffreys stood on a platform in South Africa, where thousands of amazing miracles of healing had taken place, and spoke these words before a mass of people: "Ladies and gentlemen, the world is at my feet."

Not long after that, the man who had ministered healing to literally thousands of people became ill. In Jeffreys' weakest moment, when he was weary physically and boasting pridefully that the whole world was at his feet, Satan struck him down.

While in England, I decided to visit Stephen Jeffreys, so I went to his house in a little town in Wales. When his wife opened the door, I introduced myself and she invited me in. There in a wheelchair sat a twisted, knotted form, head pulled down and feet drawn up. It was Stephen Jeffreys. To see his face, I had to kneel down before him.

Having ministered healing and deliverance to thousands, Stephen Jeffreys died of rheumatoid arthritis. When he said the world was at his feet, he was sorely mistaken. The world is at Jesus' feet.

Fred Squire

Of course many stayed humble before God. While serving as song leader for Stephen Jeffreys, Fred Squire received an anointing to minister healing. He was especially blessed in ministering to the blind. There were over 400 people whose eyes were opened in his meetings. Whenever a blind person was in one of his meetings, Fred Squire was joyous, knowing beyond doubt that he would be healed. This is one of the gifts of healing.

Jack Coe

In the early 1950s Jack Coe, an evangelist with the Assemblies of God, conducted a remarkable ministry of divine healing. I attended one of his meetings in New York City where a tent, holding over ten thousand people, was packed to capacity. That night while seated on the platform with Coe, I witnessed tremendous demonstrations of the gifts of healing. At least a dozen people rose from their wheelchairs and cots.

No doubt Jack Coe's ministry was one of the most outstanding, but he began to exalt himself. No matter how glorious his ministry was, he tried to make himself more glorious in the eyes of the people, and his life was cut short. In late 1956 while preaching in Hot Springs, Arkansas, Coe became critically ill and was later diagnosed as suffering from polio. He died early in 1957. He told Gordon

Lindsay that God was removing him from the ministry.

William Branham

Another minister of almost unbelievable miracles was William Branham. Wherever he conducted meetings in the world, phenomenal miracles took place. Not only did he possess the gifts of power, but the gifts of revelation functioned through him in a most remarkable way.

When people are gifted by the Holy Ghost in ministry, it is sometimes difficult for them to remain humble and unselfish before God. Eventually, Branham developed some doctrines that were removed from the truth. By the 1960s he was regarded as an extremely controversial teacher. In 1963 he received a "revelation" that he was one of the witnesses in the book of Revelation, chapter 11.

In December, 1965, Branham was driving cross-country to Arizona when his car was struck head-on by a drunken driver. He lay in a coma for several days until his death on Christmas Eve. For several days thereafter, some of his followers believed he would rise from the dead. One group, who believed Branham to be God, born of a virgin, was even expecting his resurrection on Easter Sunday, 1966.

Smith Wigglesworth

Smith Wigglesworth was especially blessed with a ministry to people who suffered from seizures of various kinds. When people with epilepsy were brought to his meetings, Wigglesworth knew there would be a revival because they were nearly always healed.

A number of times when people had epileptic seizures during his meetings, Wigglesworth would stop his sermon, leave the platform, minister deliverance to them, return to the platform, and continue preaching. He had no doubt that when he touched them, they would be set free — and they were!

Ways To Be Healed

Now we come to the most important aspect of this subject: the ways a person can be healed. We must always remember that there are many ways to be healed.

The greatest way to be healed is to *pray for yourself.* More people are healed by praying for themselves than all the other ways combined.

The second way is *to have a family member pray for you.* Millions of healings have been the result of mothers and fathers praying for their children. If families would develop this truth, they would not stop with their own family, but would reach out in prayer to their entire neighborhood.

Another way is to *call for the minister and elders of your church.* This biblical way is set out in James 5:14,15: *Is any sick among you? let him call for the elders of the church; and let them pray over him, anointing him with oil in the name of the Lord: And the prayer of faith shall save the sick, and the Lord shall raise him up; and if he have committed sins, they shall be forgiven him.* You are to call for the elders in the Body — spiritual leaders among your fellowship who are full of faith and full of the Word. As they lay hands on you and anoint you with oil, you will be healed.

Then there is a sign gift ministry — *the gifts of healing* — which, as we have already discussed, is a remarkable way to be healed. Through this ministry the Lord endows His servants with special gifts to pray for specific diseases. A minister does not always have to seek for a certain sign gift of healing. Many times it will be bestowed upon him in the line of ministry, and as his understanding increases, that ministry gift will also grow and increase.

The Working of Miracles

In the category of power gifts, there is the gift of the working of miracles. Regarding this gift, we must realize one thing: We are dealing with God, and it is a miracle only as far as man is concerned. Since God is omnipotent — having all power — He does not recognize a certain event as a miracle. What we consider to be a miracle is only an act of God; it is only the voice of God speaking, causing something to come to pass. What might be a very small thing in God's sight is a miracle to man because he is unable to perform it in his own natural strength.

A supernatural occurrence is called a miracle because it is beyond our natural comprehension. When we receive our glorified bodies, the acts we consider to be miracles at the present time will no longer be miracles; they will be perfectly normal.

The Lord Jesus Christ spoke to a fig tree and said, "Die." (Mark 11:12-14.) The disciples were shocked to see it withered up just the next morning. (Mark 11:20-26.) To the Lord Jesus that was a very simple thing. To the disciples it was an enormous situation, an unbelievable thing, simply because it was outside their regular operating forces and strength.

The Greek words for "working of miracles" are *energema* and *dunamis*. From the word *energema* we derive our word "energy"; from the word *dunamis* we derive our word "dynamite." *Dunamis* is the same word translated "power" in Acts 1:8. Jesus said to His disciples, *Ye shall receive power, after that the Holy Ghost is come upon you.* Thus, we can see that this gift of energy, or dynamite, is God's doing something of an explosive nature.

The gift of the working of miracles means a supernatural intervention by God in the ordinary course of nature. It is God working through a person, an animal, or some other instrument, to do something that could not be done normally.

In the first power gift — the gift of faith — God is working in our behalf, but independent of us. We do nothing. In the gift of faith God does something sovereignly, dramatically, gloriously, while we just watch and marvel. God does the work *for* us, not *through* us.

In the gift of the working of miracles the exact opposite is true. God is entrusting us with a strength, with an energy, that we do not normally have. It is the power of the Spirit of God surging through us — through our hands, our feet, our minds — causing us to do or be something that is not normal or natural to our behavior. We call this the gift of the working of miracles.

A Dumb Animal Spoke

By the working of miracles, very often the laws of nature are altered or suspended, and that which is abnormal to our natural reasoning becomes effective around us. This gift has functioned in the Bible, even through an animal, as we see in the Book of Numbers, chapter 22.

This is a very unusual story. The prophet Balaam was weak and wavering in respect to God's express will and was being tempted by the enemies of God's people.

And Balaam rose up in the morning, and saddled his ass, and went with the princes of Moab.

And God's anger was kindled because he went: and the angel of the Lord stood in the way for an adversary against him. Now he was riding upon his ass, and his two servants were with him.

And the ass saw the angel of the Lord standing in the way, and his sword drawn in his hand: and the ass turned aside out of the way, and went into the field: and Balaam smote the ass, to turn her into the way.

Numbers 22:21-23

When Balaam's donkey saw the angel of the Lord standing in the way, it turned aside into a field. Then it crushed Balaam against a wall *and finally laid down under him.* Each time Balaam punished the donkey: . . . *and Balaam's anger was kindled, and he smote the ass with a staff* (v. 27).

Then the Lord spoke through the animal and said, *What have I done unto thee, that thou hast smitten me these three times?* (v. 28).

Balaam said, . . . *Because thou hast mocked me: I would there were a sword in mine hand, for now would I kill thee* (v. 29).

Again God spoke through the animal to Balaam: *Am not I thine ass, upon which thou hast ridden ever since I was thine unto this day? was I ever wont to do so unto thee?* (v. 30).

Then God opened Balaam's eyes and he saw the angel standing in front of him with sword drawn. It was only the animal that had kept Balaam from being killed. If the animal had not held back, Balaam would have died when he ran into the two-edged sword of that angel. The animal could see it, but the prophet could not. Then God gave that animal the voice of a human. To us that is a miracle.

On this occasion the miracle that took place was not a small affair. God would not have His people cursed. Finally, out of this strange prophet's lips came these words: *How shall I curse, whom God hath not cursed? or how shall I defy, whom the Lord hath not defied?* (Num. 23:8).

Balaam was unable to compromise with the enemy, even though he was offered great treasures to do it.

Elijah

The gift of miracles is remarkably demonstrated through the prophet Elijah in 2 Kings 2:8. *And Elijah took his mantel* (which is an ordinary coat), *and wrapped it together, and smote the waters, and they were divided hither and thither, so that they two* (Elijah and Elisha) *went over on dry ground.*

When both were on the other side, the waters again flowed normally. Because Elijah used a material object — his coat — this act must be classified, not as an act of faith, but as the working of a miracle.

David

King David operated in the working of miracles. In 1 Samuel, chapter 17, he tells how he slew a lion and a bear with his naked hands:

And David said unto Saul, Thy servant kept his father's sheep, and there came a lion, and a bear, and took a lamb out of the flock; and I went out after him, and smote him, and delivered it out of his mouth; and when he arose against me, I caught him by his beard, and smote him, and slew him (vv. 34,35).

Then David proceeded to face Goliath, a Philistine who stood ten feet tall. Armed with only a stone and a sling, David slew the giant, for he had said: *The Lord that delivered me out of the paw of the lion, and out of the paw of the bear, he will deliver me out of the hand of this Philistine* (v. 37).

These acts would have to be classed as the working of miracles because David was involved in their completion. He could not kill a lion or a bear with his bare hands. For him to wrestle with a lion and win took a power that he normally did not have.

This is different from the story of Daniel in the lions' den. Daniel functioned in the gift of faith. He did not touch a lion; he trusted God. It was an angel that came and closed the jaws of the lions.

Samson

Another illustration of the working of miracles can be seen in the life of Samson. Samson was a very unusual person. Before he was born, his mother gave him to God and proclaimed him a Nazarite, which meant that he would never touch dead flesh, or drink wine, or clip his hair. (Judg. 13:5.)

The Bible says that as Samson became a young man, the Spirit of God moved upon him. (Judg. 13:25.)

. . . and, behold, a young lion roared against him. And the Spirit of the Lord came mightily upon him, and he rent him as he would have rent a kid, and he had nothing in his hand (Judg. 14:5,6).

When three thousand men came against him, he slew a thousand men with only the jawbone of an ass. (Judg. 15:14,15.)

Then, as his final act, Samson dislocated the two middle pillars of a great temple, where thousands of pagans were worshiping their god. (Judg. 16:29,30.) By pushing those pillars out of place, he destroyed more of the enemies of God at one time than he had destroyed in his whole life.

Samson possessed the gift of the working of miracles.

Jesus and the Working of Miracles

At the wedding feast in Cana of Galilee Jesus turned water into wine. (John 2:1-11.) Through the working of miracles, the laws of nature were affected: the fermenting stage was accelerated.

In Matthew 14, when Jesus broke the bread and the fishes to feed the multitude, every break was a miracle of multiplication. He took each loaf and each fish and with His natural hands kept breaking them until the disciples had enough to feed thousands of people. With little, Jesus fed many, and there were twelve baskets of leftovers! His disciples were amazed. This is the functioning of the gift of the working of miracles.

9
The Gifts of Inspiration

The third group of spiritual gifts consists of the gifts of inspiration: prophecy, tongues, and the interpretation of tongues.

Unlike the first two groups — the gifts of power and the gifts of revelation — these three gifts of inspiration are not the kind that change the world. The gifts of inspiration are strictly for the benefit of the Church. They have a threefold ministry: edification, exhortation, and comfort.

God wants His people strong and mature in spiritual matters. He wants a Church that is alive and powerful. These three gifts of inspiration were designed for that purpose.

The Gift of Prophecy

Prophecy is the greatest of the three gifts of inspiration. In 1 Corinthians, chapters 11-14, the gift of prophecy is referred to a total of 22 times, which seems to reveal its importance.

What Prophecy Is Not

The gift of prophecy is not foretelling the future. Prophecy in the New Testament is different from a prophet who foretells the future. God specifically limits this gift to three beautiful exercises — edification, exhortation, and comfort — and none of these have to do with the gifts of power or the gifts of revelation.

According to Ephesians 4:8-12, the prophet is one of the five ministry gifts given to the Church. He is a person, not a vocal gift. He holds the office of prophet. Acts 21:9 tells of Philip's four daughters

111

"which did prophesy." They were not prophets, but they prophesied. They had a ministry of edifying the Church, but they did not foretell the future.

The prophetic office *always* predicts the future; the gift of prophecy *never* predicts the future.

The gift of prophecy is not to be used for guidance. This is one of the major ways in which people have misused this gift. Guidance is not one of the three blessings of prophecy.

The gift of prophecy is not preaching. To preach means to proclaim and pronounce the Good News — the Gospel of Jesus Christ. Preaching comes from the natural mind; prophecy is the mind of the Holy Spirit speaking to us in a supernatural utterance. Preaching can be inspired or anointed, but it is not supernatural; prophecy is *always* supernatural. Prophecy is a supernatural utterance that comes from a person who is anointed to speak the treasures of God to the Body of Christ.

The gift of prophecy is not rebuke. There is no element of rebuke in prophecy; there is always encouragement. In the New Testament, correction comes, not from prophecy, but from preaching the Word with doctrine. Paul dealt with excesses as a teacher, a pastor, and an apostle, but never through the gift of prophecy.

The gift of prophecy is not a ministry of criticism. Prophecy is not one person's opinion against another. It is a divine operation under the anointing of God, designed to warn men and women of sin or shortcomings so that they might be ready when Jesus comes. The gift of prophecy can lift a Christian out of his depression, his negligence, and his lukewarmness, and put him back into the mainstream of the thrust of God.

Threefold Purpose of Prophecy

The gift of prophecy is for three reasons: edification, exhortation, and comfort.

Edification

To edify means to build up. This gift of prophecy will build up the Church of Jesus Christ. If a man is weak spiritually, it will build him up. If a woman is afraid, it will remove the fear. This gift of prophecy in its root meaning signifies to erect, to strengthen, to build up. There are multitudes of Christians today who are in great need of having their spiritual lives built up and strengthened. This is why the gifts of inspiration were given to the Church by the Holy Spirit.

In 1 Corinthians 14:18, Paul wrote: *I thank my God, I speak with tongues more than ye all.* No doubt, the reason Paul spoke in tongues more than the entire Corinthian church fellowship was his desire to be built up. This is one of the secrets of his amazing spiritual strength.

Exhortation

In exhortation we have a call to encouragement. Many times I have heard a word of prophecy that will exhort a church fellowship to holiness, consecration, and separation from the world. Many times when the Devil discourages us, this gift of prophecy will encourage us. It can bring an exhortation: "Jesus is coming soon. Don't stop here. Don't let the world come in like a flood. Keep moving with God." It exhorts us to keep ourselves built up and strong in God.

There have been times when a word of exhortation has changed my life. I could feel the Holy Spirit speaking such forceful words through a person.

Comfort

The Greek word for comfort is consolation, which would include the healing of distress, of sorrow, of persecution, and of suffering.

We live in a world of broken lives, broken homes, and broken ambitions. People today do not necessarily need sympathy or pity; they need comfort. The Church needs divine comfort from the Holy Spirit to bring heaven's healing into their hearts. It is our duty and our privilege to come to church and say, "Lord, we want the tenderest of the gifts to function. We want prophecy to function."

Some people who come to our churches are so sad; they don't know what to do. Some of them are actually contemplating suicide. If there is anything we should give these people, it is comfort — healing of the inner person, healing of the memories, healing of sadness and depression. We can do it through the praises of God and through sincere fellowship with our brothers and sisters in the Body. We can bring comfort when we shake hands with one another and embrace one another. We can say, "The Lord comfort you and bless you."

These three ministries of prophecy — edification, exhortation, and comfort — should be functioning in every prayer group and church fellowship. If prophecy is the tenderest of all the gifts, how much it should function in all our lives!

This gift is available, not to just a few, but to the total Church. Begin now by saying, "Lord, I want these gifts to function in my life." If you are sincere, God will cause these gifts to function in and through you. He wants you to be an instrument He can use to edify, exhort, and comfort His people.

Controlling the Gift of Prophecy

According to 1 Corinthians 14:32, the possessor of the gift of prophecy can control that gift: *The spirits of the prophets are subject to the prophets.* Whenever a person says of their utterances, "I can't stop doing this," you can be sure that an alien spirit is involved. At no time is a person bound by the manifestation of a spiritual gift.

This is the difference between being controlled by the Devil and being controlled by God. You can stop God and grieve the Holy Spirit at any time. You are not under bondage to the Holy Spirit. You work with Him and flow with Him because you want to. You have to keep flowing in the Spirit if you expect the gifts to operate in and through you.

First Corinthians 14:29 tells how the gift of prophecy is regulated: *Let the prophets speak two or three, and let the other judge.* There should be at the most only three messages of prophecy in one meeting. Even if you should feel a thrust to prophesy, you should control it if God has already spoken three times. The Word says that is enough for one service.

Verse 33 tells how this gift can be safeguarded and protected: *God is not the author of confusion, but of peace.*

In 1 Thessalonians 5:20 we are told plainly: *Despise not prophesyings.* Some pastors and ministers do not want the gift of prophecy to function in their churches because they cannot personally control it. When dealing with the supernatural, there is a certain element of danger involved, which is true with so many things. Driving an automobile or flying an airplane can be dangerous. Anything worth very much can be somewhat dangerous.

When the gifts of the Spirit are not functioning properly, they can be dangerous to the Church. You can have a fire in the basement of a building; but as long as the fire is inside the furnace, there is no problem. Should that fire be outside the furnace and in the center of the room, you would have trouble. Though it is the same fire, it is in the wrong place.

The gifts of the Spirit have a proper place and a proper time. To function best, they should function at that place and time.

Romans 12:6 says, *Let us prophesy according to the proportion of faith.* If a person prophesies things that do not come to pass, he is speaking beyond his faith and he should stop. The Apostle Paul wrote these words to Timothy: *Stir up the gift of God, which is in thee* (2 Tim. 1:6). No doubt the gift he was speaking of was the gift of prophecy.

Divers Kinds of Tongues

Divers kinds of tongues is a gift used for public ministry. It is a sign gift from God, a distinguishing gift that does something very particular.

Wherefore tongues are for a sign, not to them that believe, but to them that believe not: but prophesying serveth not for them that believe not, but for them which believe (1 Cor. 14:22). Tongues is for a sign to the unbeliever, to stir him inside.

Speaking with tongues as the Holy Spirit gives utterance is a unique ministry that has not been used in other dispensations. It is identified only with the Church Age, the age we are living in today.

The phenomenon of speaking in tongues began on the day of Pentecost — the day the New Testament Church was born in Jerusalem. This gift of tongues has been identified with the Church since its inception and it has not left the Church since that day. None of the nine gifts have left the Church.

This sign gift of divers kinds of tongues is a supernatural utterance, which comes from God through the Person of the Holy Spirit. This remarkable gift is directed through man's spirit and manifests as a spirit language, a divine and spiritual communication that is different from his native tongue.

Tongues is the most misunderstood of all the spiritual gifts. There is no gift in all the world that receives so explosive a reaction as the gift of tongues. Because the Devil is afraid of it, he gets everybody fighting over it. If tongues did not cause him trouble, he would ignore it, but speaking in tongues is dynamic. It will change a person's life, so Satan fights it with every force he can muster.

We need to understand it better, so we can use it more. If we are going to use the sword, we must use it with dexterity. If we are going to use this gift of tongues, we must use it mightily as unto the Lord.

What Tongues Is Not

The sign gift of tongues is not the prayer language of tongues that comes with the infilling of the Holy Spirit. It is not the receiving of the Spirit at baptism when one is "filled with the Spirit," as in Acts 2:4: *And they were all filled with the Holy Ghost, and began to speak with other tongues, as the Spirit gave them utterance.*

The gift of tongues is not the learning of languages. Tongues has positively no relationship to the thinking abilities of man. When a person speaks in tongues, he has no understanding of what he is saying. The Apostle Paul wrote: *For if I pray in an unknown tongue, my spirit prayeth, but my understanding is unfruitful* (1 Cor. 14:14). His spirit is speaking to God. *He that speaketh in an unknown tongue speaketh not unto men, but unto God* (v. 2). Tongues is speech to God — a vocal miracle. What a joy it is to speak personally and directly to the Most High God!

This means there is an element of faith and an element of courage related to this gift. You must be able to say in faith, "Lord, I believe this is You." You must be able to say with courage, "I don't care what men think; I'm going to let the blessing of God flow through me."

God wants it to flow through each one of us. The gift of tongues is a special challenge and a sign to those, the Bible says, who are uninformed.

Who Can Have the Gift of Tongues?

Only Spirit-filled, or Spirit-baptized, believers are candidates for this gift. The infilling of the Holy Spirit is the door to the operation of spiritual gifts in your life. You must pass through that door to reach all the "goodies" on the inside. Many people want these mighty gifts of the Spirit to function in their lives, but are unwilling to step through that door.

Before a person can operate this Church gift, he must first experience Acts 2:4; he must speak with tongues. In 1 Corinthians 14:5 Paul said, *I would that ye all spoke with tongues.* None of us have the right to say, "Let somebody else do it. I won't do it."

Tongues is a part of the Great Commission to the Church — the Lord Jesus Christ's last words on earth before He was taken up into heaven. He said:

Go ye into all the world, and preach the gospel to every creature.

He that believeth and is baptized shall be saved; but he that believeth not shall be damned.

And these signs shall follow them that believe; In my name shall they cast out devils; they shall speak with new tongues . . .

Mark 16:15-17

This gift was prophesied even by such a great prophet as the Lord Jesus Christ. There is no doubt or ambiguity about what Jesus said. He said exactly what He meant and meant exactly what He said! It is available to each of us.

Where Does This Gift Operate?

Tongues is a gift for the Body. First Corinthians 14:23 refers to tongues operating when the whole Church has come together into one place. Verse 26 says, . . . *when ye come together, every one of you hath a psalm, hath a doctrine, hath a tongue, hath a revelation, hath an interpretation.*

. . . *when ye come together* . . . . The gift of tongues is a come-together gift. It operates when we assemble ourselves together. However, when you use your own private prayer language, there is no need for anyone else. It is a beautiful experience you

119

can enjoy alone. When I am speaking in my prayer language, I am alone most of the time. I get more inspiration walking around by myself or driving alone in my car, talking to the Lord. It is a beautiful experience for the spiritual man.

Tongues Edify

God specifically says the vocal gifts of inspiration are designated to edify or build up the total Church of the Lord Jesus Christ. When we understand this, then every time we meet together, we can say without reservation, "Let the gifts function."

He that speaketh in an unknown tongue edifieth himself (1 Cor. 14:4). When this beautiful gift of tongues is in manifestation, it causes a building up and a strengthening within the speaker.

This gift can function in two ways: by speaking and by singing. Colossians 3:16 says, *Let the word of Christ dwell in you richly in all wisdom; teaching and admonishing one another in psalms and hymns and spiritual songs, singing with grace in your hearts to the Lord.*

This is such a beautiful verse. We are to teach and admonish one another in psalms, hymns, and spiritual songs. Have you ever thought of songs as being for teaching and admonishing? Ephesians 5:19 says, *Speaking to yourselves in psalms and hymns and spiritual songs, singing and making melody in your heart to the Lord.*

So here we find tremendous evidence of how this gift of tongues can function to the edifying and building up of the Body.

Tongues Is For Everyone

Church leaders must not forbid the use of this gift. In 1 Corinthians 14:39 Paul wrote: *Brethren, covet to prophesy, and forbid not to speak with tongues.* If the Word says, "Forbid not," I think we should be careful about what we forbid. In some areas of our world today we would be forbidden to practice this gift. Thank God, we are living in a new atmosphere in this country. Almost every denomination in America today has within it a certain segment that has been filled with the Holy Spirit.

Paul had previously stated: *I would that ye all spake with tongues* (1 Cor. 14:5). If the Word of God says all of us should have this gift, then without exception all of us should have it.

The gift of tongues should not be neglected, but it can be. It can lie dormant within us. In 1 Timothy 4:14 the Apostle Paul wrote to young Timothy: *Neglect not the gift that is in thee, which was given thee by prophecy, with the laying on of the hands of the presbytery.*

Will Tongues Cease?

Some have said that tongues will cease. *Charity never faileth: but whether there be prophecies, they shall fail: whether there be tongues, they shall cease: whether there be knowledge, it shall vanish away* (1 Cor. 13:8).

When will tongues cease? The Holy Spirit is particularly identified with the Church. Has the Church Age ended? No. There is no Bible intimation of a change to be made in Church law or policy or construction from the day the Church was born until it is raptured and taken to be with Jesus. Tongues

121

will cease, but it will not occur until the end of this age. At the same time the other gifts will cease. When the Church is with God, the gifts of the Spirit will no longer be needed.

Why Will Tongues Cease?

In heaven we will no longer need the Holy Spirit to guide us into all truth. We will speak the same language as Jesus, so the gift of tongues will not be necessary at that time.

One purpose of tongues is as a sign to the unbeliever, but there will be no unbelievers in heaven. We will no longer need unknown tongues to glorify God in heaven; there will be only one language — heaven's language — and all of us will be speaking it.

We will no longer need tongues to edify ourselves. We will be edified by being in God's presence forever, jubilant throughout all eternity!

Why Speak In Tongues?

Here are a number of reasons why Christians should speak in tongues:

1. **Tongues is evidence of the infilling of the Holy Spirit.** This is shown three times in the Acts of the Apostles: in chapter 2, on the day the Church was born; in chapter 10, about ten years later when Peter ministered to the Gentiles; in chapter 19, about twenty years later when Paul laid hands on the believers in Ephesus. In each of these passages, the Bible specifically says the people spoke with tongues.

2. **Tongues is your prayer language.** As we find in 1 Corinthians 14:2, when you speak in tongues, you

are speaking supernaturally to God. Your spirit prays, but your mind does not understand. Your spirit is the real you — your inner man — and it is that inner person (the real you) who is talking to God.

3. **With tongues, you magnify God.** To magnify God is to make Him great. *They heard them speak with tongues, and magnify God* (Acts 10:46).

4. **Tongues edifies.** First Corinthians 14:4 says, *He that speaketh in an unknown tongue edifieth himself.* When you edify yourself, you are building up spiritual strength within yourself.

5. **Tongues brings gladness in singing.** In 1 Corinthians 14:15 Paul wrote: . . . *I will sing with the spirit, and I will sing with the understanding also.* Singing with the spirit becomes a source of gladness in singing unto the Lord.

6. **Tongues is a source of intercessory prayer.** Intercessory prayer is one of the greatest spiritual undertakings. Romans 8:26 says, *The Spirit also helpeth our infirmities: for we know not what we should pray for as we ought: but the Spirit itself maketh intercession for us with groanings which cannot be uttered.* This is a different level of prayer. In the forty or fifty years of my ministry, I have experienced this type of in-depth intercessory prayer only five or six times.

7. **Tongues is a source of spiritual refreshing.** Isaiah 28:11,12 says, *For with stammering lips and another tongue will he speak to this people . . . This is the rest wherewith ye may cause the weary to rest; and this is the refreshing.* Tongues provides a spiritual stamina that comes only from God.

8. Speaking and ministering to the Lord in tongues is somewhat like a repository of profit. As is stated in 1 Corinthians 12:7, *But the manifestation of the Spirit is given to every man to profit withal.* Through tongues, God can bring into your life an enrichment and a spiritual blessing you have never known before as you realize and experience a new nearness to God.

The Interpretation of Tongues

The third gift of inspiration is the interpretation of tongues — the supernatural verbalization of the meaning of a message just delivered to the Church by a member of the Body of Christ in a language he does not understand.

The purpose of this gift is to interpret and render a message intelligible that was given forth in an unintelligible tongue. One person gives a message in a language he does not know, and another person interprets it. This reveals the presence of God in that place. God has brought to those people a very special message, calling for action.

The person who operates in the gift of tongues should seek the gift of interpretation. *Wherefore let him that speaketh in an unknown tongue pray that he may interpret* (1 Cor. 14:13). If you possess the gift of tongues and happen to be in a gathering where there is no interpreter, you should be able to interpret.

The ministry of this gift is to edify and build up the Church. When the gift of interpretation functions with its sister gift, the gift of tongues, it equals prophecy, which according to 1 Corinthians 14:4 does edify the Church.

124

Tongues and interpretation is the functioning of a miracle which can easily be observed by the unbeliever, causing consternation when it is witnessed, just as on the day of Pentecost when the Church was born.

The interpretation of tongues is not a translation. If one person gives forth a message in tongues and two different people have the interpretation, each interpretation will be different. The essence of the message, the deep root of it, will be similar; but the phrasing of it will be different because it is not a word-for-word translation. A translation is an exact rendering from one language to another in precise grammatical terms; an interpretation reveals what God wants us to know. This explains how at times a message in tongues might be long while the interpretation is short.

On some of my trips to foreign countries, there were times when I thought my interpreter was preaching his own sermon. It seemed that way because he was *interpreting* my message, not *translating* it.

The interpretation of tongues is not an operation of the human mind. It is the functioning of the Holy Spirit through the mind. The interpreter does not understand the language or the tongue that he is interpreting. His mental faculties are not a part of the message, so he has no thought in his mind as to what the Spirit is going to say. If he does, he is not interpreting by the Spirit.

I have been in foreign countries and heard a person speak. Though I did not know the language, I knew supernaturally that it was a message in tongues, so I stood up and interpreted it in English. Since no one present understood English, my interpreter had to interpret what I said into their native language. If I had not interpreted the message, it would have been lost.

When a message is given in tongues and no interpretation follows, there are two possible reasons:

1. No one present has the gift of interpretation.
2. The speaker was simply magnifying God and no public interpretation of the message was necessary.

The interpretation of tongues can come in two ways: The interpreter speaks the words inspirationally, or he sees what he is speaking about in the form of a vision.

The interpretation of tongues requires a measure of faith. The interpreter normally receives only one or two words at a time; he does not receive the complete message at once. By faith, he must give those words; and by giving those words, God gives him the next words. As he speaks, the message will continue to come a few words at a time until he is finished. Even if the message lasts thirty minutes, the interpreter gets only a few words at a time.

This Gift Illustrated

A tremendous illustration of the fruit of this gift took place when I preached in Washington, D.C. After my sermon, one brother gave a message and another interpreted. When they had finished, a young man walked to the front and spoke in a foreign language to the one who had given the message.

The brother answered, "I'm sorry, sir, but I don't understand any other language."

The man replied, "But you spoke my language beautifully. I am Persian. You spoke my language and told me that I must get right with God, that I must find God right now."

The brother answered, "No, it was the Spirit Who spoke to you. It was God talking to you, not me."

Much to that young man's surprise, neither of the two men — the one who gave the message in tongues and the one who interpreted it — spoke or understood his language. He stood there, trembling, then knelt down and gave his heart to the Lord Jesus Christ.

That night the gifts of tongues and interpretation were magnificently fulfilled. Just as the Bible says, it was a sign to the unbeliever. God spoke to that man in the Persian language through two men when neither of them understood a foreign tongue. One man was a real estate agent; the other was a car salesman.

Tongues and Interpretation — Rules of Operation

Tongues and interpretation of tongues are regulated by the Scriptures. If a fellowship of believers does not function properly in the gifts of the Spirit, those gifts will cease to function. If believers try to operate the gifts outside the bounds of the Word, they will cease. There are literally thousands of churches in our generation that at one time possessed the gifts of the Spirit to some extent; but because the people did not understand them correctly, the gifts ceased.

Tongues without interpretation is forbidden in the Church.

The Apostle Paul wrote:

I thank my God, I speak with tongues more than ye all:

Yet in the church I had rather speak five words with my understanding, that by my voice I might teach others also, than ten thousand in an unknown tongue.

1 Corinthians 14:18,19

From five words to ten thousand words is quite a jump! Paul is simply showing how meaningless it is for a person to speak out during a church service in a tongue that is not interpreted. He would rather speak only five words that had meaning than rattle off ten thousand words and not say anything that anyone could understand. He is showing the rationale of performing the gifts of the Spirit as God wants them performed.

The gift of tongues is limited in its use.

How is it then, brethren? when ye come together, every one of you hath a psalm, hath a doctrine, hath a tongue, hath a revelation, hath an interpretation. Let all things be done unto edifying.

If any man speak in an unknown tongue, let it be by two, or at the most by three, and that by course; and let one interpret.

1 Corinthians 14:26,27

As previously stated, in any service there should be a maximum of three messages given forth in an unknown tongue with an interpretation each time. I have always thought that, since heaven does things so precisely, surely the Holy Spirit can say all that needs to be said in three messages.

The reason for this is found in 1 Corinthians 14:33, which says: *God is not the author of confusion, but of peace, as in all churches of the saints.* These gifts are regulated, not by God, but by the Church.

Again verse 27 says: *If any man speak in an unknown tongue, let it be by two, or at the most by three, and that by course; and let one interpret.* In some churches I have visited, there have been two different messages in tongues and two different people giving the interpretations. The Word of God says: *Let one interpret.* Normally in a service only one person should interpret.

In Great Britain the gifts of the Spirit have been in much greater evidence than in the United States. At a conference there, the moderator will stand at the opening session and announce who will interpret during the convention. No matter who gives a message in tongues, that same person will interpret each time. Though there may be many interpreters in a church, the Bible says the same one should interpret during each individual service.

First Corinthians 14:28 says: *If there be no interpreter, let him keep silence in the church; and let him speak to himself, and to God.* This is one of the clearest manifestations of church order you will find. If there is no interpreter and the speaker does not possess the gift of interpretation, then he should keep silence in the church and speak only to himself and to God.

This proves that when we are operating in spiritual gifts, we have control over the situation.

We are not controlled by an extraneous power. According to the Bible, the Holy Spirit is a true gentleman. He will never force a person to do anything. He offers the opportunity; whether or not we take it is our choice.

In 1 Corinthians 14:29-32 we read:

Let the prophets speak two or three, and let the other judge.

If any thing be revealed to another that sitteth by, let the first hold his peace.

For ye may all prophesy one by one, that all may learn, and all may be comforted.

And the spirits of the prophets are subject to the prophets.

When anyone says, "I'm uncontrollable," he is not under the power of the Holy Spirit, but under the Devil's power.

God will not force a person to go to heaven; neither will He force a person to live right. He did not force Lucifer, the archangel, to live right when Lucifer rebelled against Him. He did not try to make Adam live right after he had sinned in the Garden of Eden. Nowhere in the Bible does God force anyone to live right.

You have to *want* to live right, and you have to *want* the gifts of the Spirit. God will not force them on you. When you do receive them, have respect for them. Learn what God has said about them; then you will have great wisdom in the operation of these gifts and they shall remain with you. There is no reason for the gifts to ever leave your life.

130

Prophecy vs. Tongues

Having studied the three inspirational gifts — prophecy, tongues, and interpretation of tongues — we will now see how these gifts function together in the Body of Christ. The Apostle Paul wrote in 1 Corinthians 14:1,2:

Follow after love, and desire spiritual gifts, but rather that ye may prophesy.

For he that speaketh in an unknown tongue speaketh not unto men, but unto God: for no man understandeth him; howbeit in the spirit he speaketh mysteries.

Paul is showing here the difference between the gift of prophecy and the gift of tongues. Together, the sister gifts of tongues and interpretation have the same message, anointing, power, and abiding presence as prophecy. They are simply two ways God has of doing the same thing. **Prophecy speaks to the people; a message in tongues speaks to God and to the sinner.**

When a person speaks in tongues, we cannot understand what is being said; in prophecy we can.

Paul continued in 1 Corinthians 14:3,4 to say:

He that prophesieth speaketh unto men to edification, and exhortation, and comfort.

He that speaketh in an unknown tongue edifieth himself; but he that prophesieth edifieth the church.

This is the basic difference in these two ministries in the Body: **Tongues edifies and builds up the speaker; prophecy builds up the Church.**

In verse 5 Paul wrote: *I would that ye all spake with tongues, but rather that ye prophesied: for greater is he that prophesieth than he that speaketh with tongues, except he interpret, that the church may receive edifying.* Prophecy and tongues are different unless there is someone present to interpret the tongues; then they become the same.

Wherefore tongues are for a sign, not to them that believe, but to them that believe not: but prophesying serveth not for them that believe not, but for them which believe (1 Cor. 14:22).

Tongues is a sign, not to the believer, but to the unbeliever. It will do amazing things for sinners. I have seen tongues and interpretation strike terror in the hearts of sinners.

Prophecy is for the Church; the edification, exhortation, and comfort of prophecy belong to God's people.

If therefore the whole church be come together into one place, and all speak with tongues, and there come in those that are unlearned, or unbelievers, will they not say that ye are mad?

But if all prophesy **(or speak out in a language all can understand)**, *and there come in one that believeth not, or one unlearned, he is convinced of all, he is judged of all:*

And thus are the secrets of his heart made manifest; and so falling down on his face he will worship God, and report that God is in you of a truth.
1 Corinthians 14:23-25

When an unbeliever comes into a group and hears these mighty words of inspiration flowing forth, he will recognize that God is present and among those people. The words they are speaking are supernatural words, not coming forth from the natural flow of their minds. The sinner will know that, and he will identify the power of God in their midst.

10
The Gifts in Jesus' Ministry

Jesus Christ came to this world for one reason: to redeem it from sin. *God so loved the world, that he gave his only begotten Son, that whosoever believeth in him should not perish, but have everlasting life* (John 3:16).

Christ came to conquer this world, to snatch it out of the hands of the Devil and save us from hell. When Jesus appeared to the Apostle John on the Isle of Patmos, He proclaimed that the keys of death and hell were in His hand. (Rev. 1:18.) Just after His resurrection, He told His disciples: *All power is given unto me in heaven and in earth* (Matt. 28:18). That means there is total victory for the Body of Christ. As a sideline to this, we have been given the gifts of the Spirit as an aid in winning the world to the Lord Jesus Christ.

Our Example in the Gifts

Some people have the idea that everything Jesus did was because He was God, but they are 100% wrong! The amazing ministry of Jesus Christ is a perfect example of a ministry that functioned within the framework of the gifts of the Spirit. If Jesus had performed His earthly ministry because He was God, then you and I could not follow His example because we are not God. But the remarkable thing is that He confined His ministry within the framework of the gifts of the Spirit.

I use the word "confined" because, as the Son of God, Jesus was not required to operate in this framework. He did not have to function through the gifts of the Holy Spirit. He could have chosen another way. As God, He could have spoken worlds into existence as was done in the beginning. (Gen. 1.) But He deliberately confined Himself to minister within the limits of the gifts of the Spirit, and He did so for one purpose: that He might be a perfect example to you and me.

If what Jesus did, He did because He was the Son of Man and used the Holy Spirit to do it, then you and I can do it, too. If the ministry of Jesus was directed, guided, and energized by the Holy Ghost, then we can have the same kind of ministry because we have the same Holy Ghost.

We can do the same works Jesus did. Jesus said in John 14:12, *He that believeth on me, the works that I do shall he do also; and greater works than these shall he do; because I go unto my Father.* That is hard to believe, but Jesus said it. These "greater works" cannot be greater in *quality*; they can only be greater in *quantity*.

He was saying to His disciples, "Greater works than these shall you do because I am only one person; you are twelve." And He sent them out to do the same works He did. You and I today are part of these "greater works."

It should give you courage and strength to know that you are part of the great things God wants to do in the earth. We are a blessed people to be alive during this time. I am so glad that God permitted me to live and minister today.

Jesus functioned under the nine gifts that are in the New Testament — so can we. These gifts of the Holy Spirit are the weapons of our warfare — the instruments we fight and win with. They are our victory instruments. Had Christ performed His ministry as God, being the Son of God, all of us would have been eliminated because we are not God.

If these gifts of the Spirit were for Paul, Peter, Moses, David, Elijah, and Daniel — but not for us today — I would not have the courage to share these things with you. But I have the courage because I know beyond the shadow of a doubt that we can have what Moses and Elijah had; we can do what Peter and Paul did. If these men had done those works because they were specially selected by God to do them, then no ordinary Christian could hope to follow such a pattern. Their stories would be only a divine record that we could read and marvel about. But the same power that was in them is available to you and me. The works that they did, we can do today.

In our generation we can do the same works as Moses, as David, as Daniel — and as Jesus. Why? Because we have the same power of God and the same anointing of the Holy Spirit motivating us that motivated them. This is the purpose of this book. I know that He, Who was, is. I know that He, Who is, will be. There are no yesterdays and there are no tomorrows, because He is the mighty I AM!

Greater Works Than These Shall Ye Do

Let me give you an example to illustrate my point.

When I was in the Philippines, God gave us a phenomenal revival. The superintendent of the Methodist church, Rubin Candalaria, came and asked if he could help me. As superintendent of the churches in the Manila area, he could gain entrance into every church, so we were able to minister in fifty different churches. There may never have been a city so ready for revival as Manila was. Night after night we went into churches of all denominations.

The move of the Spirit was so grand and so beautiful. Such remarkable things took place. The first night in the great Knox Memorial Church, the oldest Protestant church in the country, the entire deacon board knelt at the altar and accepted Jesus Christ as their Lord and Savior.

When I could not keep an appointment at a certain church, I said to Rubin Candalaria, "You go in my place."

He turned pale and said, "I can't do that!"

"But you have to do it. The meeting is announced and the people can't be disappointed."

He kept saying, "I can't."

"Why can't you?"

"I have been with you all these months. After every service you lay hands on everyone who wants to be prayed for. I have witnessed hundreds of miracles take place. It would not be right for me to go before them. *I don't have any power to help them.*"

I said, "If you knew you had the power of God to do it, would you do it?"

He said, "Yes." Before you could count to three, I grabbed him and prayed the anointing of the Holy Ghost on him. Then I said, "Go quickly!" He went, and has been going ever since! You can do the same!

The Gifts As They Functioned in Jesus

We would expect the gifts of the Spirit to be manifested in the ministry of Jesus. Our only problem would be in identifying them and describing how they functioned in His life. Let's identify some of them now.

The Word of Wisdom

In Matthew's Gospel, chapter 24, Jesus predicted the future. He said that false Christs and false Messiahs would come; that there would be wars and rumors of wars; that there would be famines, pestilences, and earthquakes. (vv. 5-7.) He said there would be great tribulation such as the world has never seen. (vv. 21,22.) He said the sun would be darkened and the moon would not give her light. (v. 29.) He said the Son of man would return just as He had gone away. (v. 30.)

Jesus was projecting the future, functioning not as God, but as a Spirit-anointed man through the gift of the word of wisdom.

Most of these events have not yet come to pass. After 2,000 years they are standing as the words of eternal life because of the word of God's wisdom.

The Word of Knowledge

An example of the gift of the word of knowledge operating in the ministry of the Lord Jesus Christ can be seen in John 1:45-50. When Jesus saw Nathanael walking toward Him, He said, *Behold an Israelite indeed, in whom is no guile!*

Nathanael responded, *Whence knowest thou me?* (In other words, "How can you call me a good man? How do you know me?")

Jesus answered and said unto him, Before that Philip called thee, when thou wast under the fig tree, I saw thee. He knew who Nathanael was and where he was. He identified him through the word of God's

137

knowledge. Supernaturally, the Lord Jesus Christ saw Nathanael the day before, sitting under a fig tree. This was a word of God's knowledge to Nathanael, and it made a believer out of him!

Nathanael answered and saith unto him, Rabbi, thou art the Son of God; thou art the King of Israel.

Jesus answered and said unto him, Because I said unto thee, I saw thee under the fig tree, believest thou? thou shalt see greater things than these.

The Discerning of Spirits

Again, we can use Nathanael as an example. When Jesus saw Nathanael, He said, *Behold an Israelite indeed, in whom is no guile!* He recognized a holy spirit within Nathanael, a man He had never before laid eyes on.

Many times Jesus discerned what was in the hearts of the people that were around Him. This was a functioning of the gift of the discerning of spirits.

In John 6:61 Jesus *knew in himself* that the disciples were murmuring. He knew the hearts of all men, which was the gift of discerning of spirits in operation. He knew the hearts of people because He discerned what was inside them. There are many evidences of this. In Luke 11 when a Pharisee invited Him to dinner, Jesus discerned what the man was thinking within himself regarding the fact that Jesus did not wash His hands before dinner.

The Gift of Faith

Jesus spoke to a fig tree and cursed it. He said, *Let no fruit grow on thee henceforward for ever* (Matt. 21:19). Then He went on His way. The next day as they passed by, the disciples saw that the fig tree had died.

138

The Gifts in Jesus' Ministry

We often ask: "Why did the Lord do this?" Because that particular type of tree always bore fruit before it had leaves. When Jesus said that it had leaves but no fruit, He saw it as a hypocrite, so He cursed it. This only reveals to us how much the Lord Jesus Christ despises hypocrisy.

Here we see the functioning of the gift of faith. Jesus never touched the tree with His hands; He merely spoke a word. By the next day, the tree had died, withered up from the roots. The gift of faith — a faith that was pungent, powerful, and demanding — said, "Die!" and that is exactly what happened.

We also see this gift demonstrated in Jesus during storms at sea. (Mark 4:37-41; Luke 8:23-25.) The Lord spoke one word to the tempestuous waves, to the thunderings in the heavens, and to the blowing winds. One word is all He needed: *Peace!* He did not say to His disciples, "Get your oars, boys, and let's see if we can equalize this thing." He said, *Peace, be still,* and at His words all those billowing waves suddenly became like a glassy sea.

Again the disciples were amazed: *What manner of man is this, that even the wind and the sea obey him?* (Mark 4:41). He did all of this with no strength pouring forth from His natural being. It was the force and pungency of a gift called faith.

The Working of Miracles

We can see the working of miracles function many times in the Lord Jesus Christ. When He laid His hands on blind eyes, something flowed through Him into that person and those eyes were opened. He raised up cripples with a hand. He took bread from a little boy, broke it, and began to fill enough baskets to feed thousands of people.

The Gifts of Healing

Christ began His ministry by demonstrating the gifts of healing. According to Matthew's Gospel, His first healing was the healing of a leper:

And, behold, there came a leper and worshipped him, saying, Lord, if thou wilt, thou canst make me clean.

And Jesus put forth his hand, and touched him, saying, I will; be thou clean. And immediately his leprosy was cleansed.

Matthew 8:2,3

In the same chapter Jesus continues His ministry by healing Peter's wife's mother of an incurable fever. (vv. 14,15.) Then they brought to Him *many that were possessed with devils: and he cast out the spirits with his word, and healed all that were sick* (v. 16).

During the ministry of Jesus Christ, healing was a top priority. His total life was dedicated to alleviating misery and hurt and pain from the human race. I believe that healing is also the ministry of the Body of Christ today. Every Christian should be praying for somebody every day. Jesus had compassion on the sick; and you can have compassion, too. Just pray for everybody you find that is sick.

The Gift of Prophecy

In the life of the Lord Jesus Christ, the gift of prophecy can be seen in the Sermon on the Mount from Matthew's Gospel, chapters 5-7. The words poured from Him with such magnificence. Many of

His utterances were purely a result of the gift of prophecy.

Tongues and Interpretation of Tongues

The gift of tongues and the gift of interpretation of tongues were actually born with the Church. It was not yet time for their function and operation during Jesus' ministry.

11
The Gifts in the Early Church

Thus far in this study on the gifts of the Holy Spirit, we have dealt with the doctrine of the gifts. We have defined each gift in simple terms and discussed how each works. Now we come to one of the most exciting portions of the entire study: the gifts of the Spirit as they operated in the early Church.

The Lord Jesus Christ said to His disciples:

Nevertheless I tell you the truth; It is expedient for you that I go away: for if I go not away, the Comforter will not come unto you; but if I depart, I will send him unto you . . .

Howbeit when he, the Spirit of truth, is come, he will guide you into all truth: for he shall not speak of himself; but whatsoever he shall hear, that shall he speak: and he will shew you things to come.

He shall glorify me: for he shall receive of mine, and shall shew it unto you. All things that the Father hath are mine: therefore said I, that he shall take of mine, and shall shew it unto you.

John 16:7,13-15

This was magnificently demonstrated in the Old Testament when Abraham (a type of our heavenly Father) desired a bride for his only son, Isaac. Abraham sent Eliezer, the chief steward of his house (a type of the Holy Spirit), into a far land to get a bride for Isaac. When Rebekah, the bride, was brought back by Eliezer, she was decorated with gifts.

As the New Testament Church — the Bride of Christ — we have been presented with gifts by the

Holy Spirit. We must exercise these gifts to the very fullest.

In Acts 1:8 the Lord Jesus said: *Ye shall receive power, after that the Holy Ghost is come upon you.* Power has to do with two elements: authority and energy. We sometimes see power only as energy, but this is not fully true. Power is also authority. When God spoke the worlds into existence, He did not use energy; He used authority — the authority of His Word. He spoke and worlds came into being. (Heb. 11:3.)

By the significance of a spoken word we, too, can speak things into existence. That is power! The source of this power is the Holy Spirit, and you receive that power when the Holy Spirit comes to rest upon you.

In Matthew's Gospel, chapter 16, the Lord Jesus was talking with His disciples — the first buds of the Great Church to be born on the day of Pentecost. In verse 15 Jesus asked: *Whom say ye that I am?*

Simon Peter answered and said, *Thou art the Christ, the Son of the living God* (v. 16).

Then Jesus said to Peter: *Blessed art thou, Simon Bar-jona: for flesh and blood hath not revealed it unto thee, but my Father which is in heaven . . . Thou art Peter, and upon this rock I will build my church; and the gates of hell shall not prevail against it* (vv. 17,18).

If we are going to win a tremendous battle, we must have weapons and armor. The gifts of the Holy Spirit are the weapons of our warfare which the gates of hell cannot prevail against. We can break down nations through the gifts of the Holy Spirit.

As was previously stated, the ministry of the Lord Jesus Christ was the embodiment of these gifts. The power of His ministry did not stem from the fact that He was the Son of God; it was because the Holy Spirit rested upon Him.

Again I quote Jesus' words in John 14:12: *He that believeth on me, the works that I do shall he do also; and greater works than these shall he do; because I go unto my Father.* Jesus could not have spoken these words in sincerity had such gifts not been made available to you and me. We draw our power from the same Source as the Lord Jesus: the Holy Spirit of God. We can have the same Source of strength He had. We can deliver to the people the same kind of authority and blessing He did.

Jesus said that even the gates of hell — the greatest force the Devil has — cannot hold up against the power of the Church. We can take the weapons of our warfare and give the Devil a good beating with them!

The Acts of the Apostles records the actual history of the infant Christian Church. It presents the early Church as it progressed for one generation, its first 33 years. If you have any question concerning the early Church, the first thing you should do is read the Acts of the Apostles. God may have put the answer to your question within those pages.

The New Testament Church began with only eleven disciples. (Of the original twelve, one was lost: Judas Iscariot.) By the day of Pentecost, there were 120. From that moment there began the greatest spiritual upheaval ever recorded by man. History has never known a period of time like those years following the day of Pentecost. Of the early Christian Church, it was written: *... These that have turned the world upside down are come hither also* (Acts 17:6). Any people who have gained that kind of publicity and notoriety deserve to be studied at length.

How did they do it? Did they start a Bible school? Did they get a good advertising scheme? Did they hire a good public relations man? We can see how people are trying to do it today; let's see how they did it then — how the Gospel grew from an infant on the day of Pentecost to a Church that encompassed the world in only one generation.

There have been great revivals and great spiritual leaders. Martin Luther changed a continent by the force and strength of one Bible truth: *The just shall live by faith* (Rom. 1:17). John Wesley moved not only the continent of Europe, but the United States as well. John Knox moved the country of Scotland to God as he created what is known today as the Presbyterian church.

But for the greatest spiritual revolution in history, we cannot speak of those times; we must return to the day of Pentecost when the power of God was demonstrated with fire and with wind. The beginning of the Christian Church was more dramatic than any revival ever held on the face of this earth. It circumnavigated the then-known world.

We need to know how it was done. Was there a specific pattern that we could follow — a pattern in the Word of God that perhaps has been hidden from us through the traditions of denominationalism? What makes the Acts of the Apostles — that fifth book of the New Testament — so outstanding? What makes it one of the most exciting books on the face of the earth?

In the city of Manila, I bought 10,000 copies of the Acts of the Apostles just to give away in my local crusade. I wanted so much for those people to read the Acts of the Infant Church. I purchased these from the Bible Society in Manila. Never before in the history of the Bible Society had anyone purchased 10,000 copies of the Acts of the Apostles. I took them to my meetings and gave them away. It was a joy!

The Infant Church

The Infant Church, born in Jerusalem, went forth to challenge and defy the entire Roman Empire with all its paganism, sensualism, witchcraft, and military might. Rome fell, but that little Church marches on!

The Infant Church defied atheistic Athens with all its philosophical might, where the mighty brains of the Grecian Empire wrote their scripts. Standing on Mars Hill, the Apostle Paul boldly proclaimed the existence of a true and living God, Who changed the lives of men. (Acts 17:22-31.)

The Infant Church emerged to convert the untutored barbarian, living in a primitive hut and held in the clutches of the awful forces of witchcraft. To him, the Church said, "We will change you, transform you, make you a person you have never been before."

The Infant Church had turned the world upside down. They were world-changers, but they did not change the world through intellectualism or by military might. They changed the world with the gifts of the Holy Ghost. The early Church knew what a battle was. It knew the issues of the battle and used only the weapons that would bring victory — the gifts of the Spirit.

The Gifts in the Church

I believe that the divine pattern for spiritual growth and direction is found in the Acts of the Apostles. In this one little book there are over fifty instances of the gifts of the Spirit in operation.

When the book of Acts was written, there were no chapter divisions. It was one continuous letter, filled with the function and operation of the Holy Ghost, giving a true picture of the Church as it is supposed to be — a church filled with love.

The gifts of the Spirit never function selfishly. They always function for the benefit of the Body of the Lord Jesus Christ. They function to bless others. As they operate through you, you will receive a blessing, but most of the blessing will belong to those around you.

Prophetically speaking, we are living at the very end of this dispensation, and it will terminate like it began — with a glorious outburst of the mighty power of God; and the gifts of the Spirit will be in full manifestation, just as they were in the early Church. If you will follow what God has placed in the book of Acts, you will know how to handle the gifts of the Holy Ghost like a veteran.

The gifts of the Spirit functioned through the Lord Jesus Christ in Acts, chapter 1. He spoke the word of wisdom to His disciples in these two instances:

The Gifts in the Early Church

. . . And, being assembled together with them, (Jesus) commanded them that they should not depart from Jerusalem, but wait for the promise of the Father, which, saith he, ye have heard of me.

For John truly baptized with water; but ye shall be baptized with the Holy Ghost not many days hence.

Acts 1:4,5

But ye shall receive power, after that the Holy Ghost is come upon you: and ye shall be witnesses unto me both in Jerusalem, and in all Judaea, and in Samaria, and unto the uttermost part of the earth.

Acts 1:8

The promise of the Holy Spirit being poured out in the city of Jerusalem at Pentecost was a prediction of what was to come: The gifts of the Holy Spirit would be poured out and the Church would be born by the power of the Holy Spirit. This was a word of God's divine wisdom, and it functioned through our Lord and Savior, Jesus Christ.

In Acts 1:11 the gift of wisdom functioned through an angel. After Jesus was taken up to heaven in a cloud, an angel appeared to the disciples and said:

Ye men of Galilee, why stand ye gazing up into heaven? this same Jesus, which is taken up from you into heaven, shall so come in like manner as ye have seen him go into heaven.

This was a word of God's wisdom. The angel was speaking of the future, an event that has not yet come to pass. It still stands as one of the gifts of the word of God's wisdom that projects the future.

In Acts 2:4 the gift of tongues functioned at least through the 120 disciples that are identified, and possibly through the whole 3,000 souls who joined the Church that day. (v. 41.)

In Acts 2:39 the word of wisdom functioned through the Apostle Peter: *For the promise is unto you, and to your children, and to all that are afar off, even as many as the Lord our God shall call.*

Acts 2:43 says: *. . . and many wonders and signs were done by the apostles.* This must have involved prophecy, healing, and miracles, though it could have included all nine gifts of the Spirit.

In Acts, chapter 3, we see the functioning of the gifts of healing through the Apostle Peter as a lame man was healed at the gate of the temple:

Peter, fastening his eyes upon him with John, said, Look on us. And he gave heed unto them, expecting to receive something of them.

Then Peter said, Silver and gold have I none; but such as I have give I thee: In the name of Jesus Christ of Nazareth rise up and walk.

And he took him by the right hand, and lifted him up: and immediately his feet and ankle bones received strength. And he leaping up stood, and walked, and entered with them into the temple, walking, and leaping, and praising God.

Acts 3:4-8

In Acts, chapter 4, the gift of faith functioned through the body of believers as they *lifted up their voice to God with one accord* and prayed: *. . . that with all boldness they may speak thy word, by stretching forth thine hand to heal; and that signs and wonders may be done by the name of thy holy* *child Jesus* (vv. 29,30). When they finished praying, *. . . the place was shaken where they were assembled together; and they were all filled with the Holy Ghost, and they spake the word of God with boldness* (v. 31).

In Acts, chapter 5, the gift of discerning of spirits functioned through Peter as Ananias and his wife Sapphira tried to deceive the apostles. When Ananias and Sapphira came to the apostles, the gift of discerning of spirits functioned and Peter knew all the secrets of their hearts. Peter said: *Ananias, why hath Satan filled thine heart to lie to the Holy Ghost, and to keep back part of the price of the land? . . . why hast thou conceived this thing in thine heart? thou hast not lied unto me, but unto God* (vv. 3,4). *And Ananias hearing these words fell down, and gave up the ghost* (v. 5).

In Acts 5:12 we read: *And by the hands of the apostles were many signs and wonders wrought among the people; (and they were all with one accord in Solomon's porch . . .).* The gift of the working of miracles was functioning and all the apostles were taking part.

In Acts 5:15,16 the gifts of healing were in operation through Peter: *. . . they brought forth the sick into the streets, and laid them on beds and couches, that at the least the shadow of Peter passing by might overshadow some of them. There came also a multitude out of the cities round about unto Jerusalem, bringing sick folks, and them which were vexed with unclean spirits: and they were healed every one.*

In Acts 5:17-20 the gift of the working of miracles functioned through an angel. When the apostles were thrown in jail, *the angel of the Lord by night opened the prison doors, and brought them forth* (v. 19).

Both the working of miracles and the gifts of healing functioned through Stephen: *And Stephen, full of faith and power, did great wonders and miracles among the people* (Acts 6:8). A vital point here is that Stephen was not an apostle, but a deacon in the Church.

Acts 8:6,7 shows how the gifts of healing and the working of miracles were demonstrated in the life of Philip, another deacon of the Church: *And the people with one accord gave heed unto those things which Philip spake, hearing and seeing the miracles which he did. For unclean spirits, crying with loud voice, came out of many that were possessed with them: and many taken with palsies, and that were lame, were healed.*

Verse 13 also refers to the working of miracles through Philip: *Then Simon himself believed also: and when he was baptized, he continued with Philip, and wondered, beholding the miracles and signs which were done.*

In verse 39 the working of miracles again operated in Philip's behalf: *And when they were come up out of the water, the Spirit of the Lord caught away Philip, that the eunuch saw him no more: and he went on his way rejoicing.*

In Acts 9:1-9 the working of miracles took place as Jesus appeared to Saul of Tarsus on the road to Damascus. In verse 6 Jesus spoke a word of wisdom to Saul: *Arise, and go into the city, and it shall be told thee what thou must do.*

The Gifts in the Early Church

Acts 9:17,18 demonstrates the gifts of healing through a disciple named Ananias, who laid hands on Saul of Tarsus that he might receive his sight.

In verse 34 Peter operated in the gifts of healing as a man sick of the palsy was raised up; and in verse 40 he ministered healing to a disciple in Joppa who had died.

In Acts 10:1-8 the gift of the word of knowledge operated through an angel. Then in verse 19 the word of knowledge came through Peter: *While Peter thought on the vision, the Spirit said unto him, Behold, three men seek thee. Arise therefore, and get thee down, and go with them, doubting nothing: for I have sent them.*

Verses 44-46 tell how the gift of tongues manifested after Peter had spoken the Gospel to a group of Gentiles.

In Acts 12:5-7 the gift of faith operated for the believers by the power and strength of an angel as Peter was set free from prison: *Peter therefore was kept in prison: but prayer was made without ceasing of the church unto God for him . . . And, behold, the angel of the Lord came upon him, and a light shined in the prison: and he smote Peter on the side, and raised him up, saying, Arise up quickly. And his chains fell off from his hands.*

We see the gift of prophecy functioning in Acts 13:1-3 as the prophets and teachers in Antioch ministered to the Lord and fasted. *As they ministered to the Lord, and fasted, the Holy Ghost said, Separate me Barnabas and Saul for the work whereunto I have called them* (v. 2).

In verses 9-11 there was the gift of the working of miracles by Paul as Elymas the Sorcerer was struck blind for standing against the Gospel.

We see the gift of the working of miracles by the Apostle Paul in Acts 14:8-10: *And there sat a certain man at Lystra, impotent in his feet, being a cripple from his mother's womb, who never had walked: the same heard Paul speak: who steadfastly beholding him, and perceiving that he had faith to be healed, said with a loud voice, Stand upright on thy feet. And he leaped and walked.*

In verses 19,20 we see the gift of the working of miracles by the disciples after Paul had been stoned and left for dead outside the city. *Howbeit, as the disciples stood round about him, he rose up, and came into the city: and the next day he departed with Barnabas to Derbe* (v. 20).

Acts, chapter 16, shows the gift of discerning of spirits through the power and anointing of the Holy Spirit when Paul was *forbidden of the Holy Ghost to preach the word in Asia.* (v. 6.)

Verse 9 is the word of wisdom to Paul: *And a vision appeared to Paul in the night: there stood a man of Macedonia, and prayed him, saying, Come over into Macedonia, and help us.*

Verse 18 shows the gift of discerning of spirits by Paul: *. . . But Paul, being grieved, turned and said to the spirit, I command thee in the name of Jesus Christ to come out of her. And he came out the same hour.*

In verses 25,26 the gift of faith and the working of miracles was demonstrated by Paul and Silas: *And at midnight Paul and Silas prayed, and sang praises unto God: and the prisoners heard them. And suddenly there was a great earthquake, so that the foundations of the prison were shaken: and immediately all the doors were opened, and everyone's bands were loosed.*

In Acts 18:9,10 we see the gift of the word of knowledge to Paul from the Lord Jesus: *Then spake the Lord to Paul in the night by a vision, Be not afraid, but speak, and hold not thy peace: for I am with thee, and no man shall set on thee to hurt thee: for I have much people in this city.*

In Acts 19:1-7 there is the demonstration of tongues and prophecy as the Holy Spirit functioned through twelve disciples in the city of Ephesus.

Verses 11,12 tell of the gifts of healing through the hands of the Apostle Paul: *And God wrought special miracles by the hands of Paul: so that from his body were brought unto the sick handkerchiefs or aprons, and the diseases departed from them, and the evil spirits went out of them.*

The gift of the working of miracles operated through Paul in Acts 20:7-12 as a young man was raised from the dead after falling from a third-story window.

Verse 22 shows the gift of the word of wisdom being activated in Paul when he said: *And now, behold, I go bound in the spirit unto Jerusalem, not knowing the things that shall befall me there.*

In Acts 21:8,9 we see the gift of prophecy through the four daughters of Philip: *. . . and we entered into the house of Philip the evangelist . . . And the same man had four daughters, virgins, which did prophesy.*

In verse 11 a prophet called Agabus spoke a word of wisdom: *And when he was come unto us, he took Paul's girdle, and bound his own hands and feet, and said, Thus saith the Holy Ghost, So shall the Jews at Jerusalem bind the man that owneth this girdle, and shall deliver him into the hands of the Gentiles.*

Paul received a word of wisdom through the Lord Jesus in Acts 22:17-21. Verse 18 says: *Make haste, and get thee quickly out of Jerusalem: for they will not receive thy testimony concerning me.*

In Acts 23:11 the word of wisdom came again to Paul through the Lord, revealing the future: *Be of good cheer, Paul: for as thou hast testified of me in Jerusalem, so must thou bear witness also at Rome.* Did it come to pass? It did! From all natural evidence, it seemed certain that Paul would die in Jerusalem, but he was delivered.

Again the gift of the word of wisdom was manifest through Paul in Acts 27:21,22: *But after long abstinence Paul stood forth in the midst of them, and said, Sirs, ye should have hearkened unto me, and not have loosed from Crete, and to have gained this harm and loss. And now I exhort you to be of good cheer; for there shall be no loss of any man's life among you, but of the ship.*

In Acts 28:3-6 there is the gift of the working of miracles through the Apostle Paul:

And when Paul had gathered a bundle of sticks, and laid them on the fire, there came a viper out of the heat, and fastened on his hand.

And when the barbarians saw the venomous beast hang on his hand, they said among themselves, No doubt this man is a murderer, whom, though he hath escaped the sea, yet vengeance suffereth not to live.

And he shook off the beast into the fire, and felt no harm. Howbeit they looked when he should have swollen, or fallen down dead suddenly, but after they had looked a great while, and saw no harm come to him, they changed their minds, and said that he was a god.

The Apostle Paul operated in the gifts of healing in Acts 28:7-9. *And it came to pass, that the father of Publius lay sick of a fever and of a bloody flux: to whom Paul entered in, and prayed, and laid his hands on him, and healed him. So when this was done, others also, which had diseases in the island, came, and were healed* (vv. 8,9).

If we could add one more to this list, it would be found in Acts, chapter 29; but there is no 29th chapter of Acts in the Bible. I am referring to *your* Acts — you are part of Acts 29. The Acts of the Apostles is a book with no termination, no conclusion. It is still being written today.

In the Acts of the Apostles we have truth. In the Acts of the Apostles we see the Church being born, springing full grown upon the stage of human events. With the Great Commission before her, she went forth to conquer the world, to revolutionize Caesar's empire, to fight against the mighty philosophies of Greece. Finally, of her, those grand words were spoken: *These that have turned the world upside down are come hither also* (Acts 17:6). It was not that a visitor had come or that a creed had come; it was a people who had turned the world upside down!

157

The gifts of the Spirit met human needs in the early Church. Wherever there were people, these gifts helped resolve their needs.

It was the power of the Holy Spirit that changed Peter from a backslider to an aggressive witness for the Lord Jesus Christ. Until he received the gift of the Holy Ghost, Peter was vacillating, shifting from one side to the other. But on the day of Pentecost, he stood before the people and boldly proclaimed the truth of the Gospel.

It was the Holy Ghost that changed Thomas from an unbelieving, doubting person to a person who was strong with living faith.

It was the Holy Ghost that changed James and John from power seekers, who wanted a throne on each side of Jesus, to humble and anointed men. (Mark 10:35-37.)

It was the power of the Holy Ghost that drove Jesus' disciples to the ends of the earth, witnessing for their Lord and Savior.

In Acts 24 Paul was given wisdom to answer the infidels in Caesar's diplomatic court. In Acts 17 he was given wisdom to answer the Stoic and Epicurean philosophers in Athens to whom everything was god. They had even erected an altar for the worship of "The Unknown God."

The strongest forces of that day, forged by the evil of the Devil, could not stand before the Church. The ingenious minds of perverted men could not control its power. Armies could not destroy it. Parliaments could not enforce laws against it. Legislators could not pass edicts to stop it. The world

158

was facing a power it could not deal with: the power of Almighty God!

A Gift Unrecalled

The Lord Jesus Christ wants His Church to receive the maximum of His love and of His gifts. There is no record in the Acts of the Apostles where the gifts of the Holy Spirit went out of commission. According to Peter's speech on the day of Pentecost, *the promise (the gift of the Holy Ghost) is unto you, and to your children, and to all that are afar off, even as many as the Lord our God shall call* (Acts 2:39). The call of God is the call to repentance, the call to salvation, so as long as God is saving people, He is still giving them the gifts of the Holy Spirit.

The Church today is right on schedule in the divine pattern to get the gifts of the Spirit functioning in their fullness. That last unfinished chapter of Acts is still being written.

12
The Gifts in the Apostle Paul

The Apostle Paul very definitely possessed and demonstrated the gifts of the Spirit in his ministry. It was Paul who brought to the Church the amazing revelation of these gifts. Perhaps it was during the three years he spent in Arabia that he delved so deeply into the mysteries of God.

This was true of Howard Carter, who often said that had he not spent World War I in prison as a conscientious objector, the world would never have had the truth of the doctrine we know today as the gifts of the Holy Spirit.

Until that time the whole Church accepted them only as natural gifts. They never said "gift of the word of wisdom," only "gift of wisdom." Instead of "word of knowledge," they said only "knowledge." To them knowledge was a human accumulation of facts; therefore, a man who knew much had the gift of knowledge. It was Mr. Carter who established these as supernatural sign gifts.

It was Paul who numbered the gifts at nine, which was a sign of their divinity and perfection. Everything God does is branded with a three. Not only did Paul number the gifts, he named them as well. Then in 1 Corinthians, chapter 14, he laid down laws regulating them. He also told us how we should seek after them. The principle in truth is reaching to receive them.

Paul was not just a teacher, a preacher, or a writer; he was a possessor of great truth. Because of this, we should expect to observe the manifestation of these gifts of the Holy Spirit in his personal ministry. How could he have the doctrine of the gifts without having the fruit of them? Let's look at some of these gifts and see how they functioned for him.

The Word of Wisdom

We can see the word of wisdom functioning many times in Paul's life. In Acts 27:10,22 he forecast the wreckage of the ship upon which he was riding, but he also forecast that no one aboard ship would be lost. To say such things on a bright sunshiny day is one thing. To say it in a storm when the ship is falling to pieces is another thing entirely. Paul was operating the gift of the word of wisdom.

In his writings to Timothy and to the Thessalonian church, Paul related the signs of the times — events that would come to pass in the last days. In 1 Timothy 4:1 he said: *The Spirit speaketh expressly, that in the latter times some shall depart from the faith, giving heed to seducing spirits, and doctrines of devils.* He said this would happen, not in his time, but in latter times. Today we are living in those latter times. Multitudes have left the faith and given heed to seducing spirits and doctrines of devils.

Just recently while I was in the St. Louis airport, a very handsome young man approached me, held out a book, and said, "May I give you this?" Immediately, I saw that it was Hinduism, a religion that originates in demon worship. This was a very fine-looking man, not peculiar in any way; yet he was seeking to convert us to paganism in our own country. Paul told us these things would take place: that many would forsake the faith and give heed to seducing spirits and doctrines of devils.

The Discerning of Spirits

In Acts, chapter 16, we see Paul manifesting the gift of discerning of spirits:

And it came to pass, as we went to prayer, a certain damsel possessed with a spirit of divination met us, which brought her masters much gain by soothsaying:

The same followed Paul and us, and cried, saying, These men are the servants of the most high God, which shew unto us the way of salvation (vv. 16,17).

But Paul looked inside her and saw an evil spirit. Finally, he turned and said to that spirit: *I command thee in the name of Jesus Christ to come out of her. And he came out the same hour* (v. 18).

In the same chapter, Acts 16, we read: *And a vision appeared to Paul in the night; there stood a man of Macedonia, and prayed him, saying, Come over into Macedonia, and help us* (v. 9). Paul discerned in his spirit that someone in Macedonia was open to the Gospel, so he immediately went there to find that open door. God gave him abundant entrance into Europe. Macedonia became Greece, so the Gospel began there and spread across to Rome.

Acts 18:19 says of Paul: *He came to Ephesus, and left them there: but he himself entered into the synagogue, and reasoned with the Jews.* Paul knew exactly what those people needed, and he poured out God's truth to them. They were amazed that out of this man was coming forth such knowledge of them. He knew their needs, their problems, and their sorrows; but he also knew what to do about it. That knowledge and discernment was pouring forth from his innermost being.

Acts 13 gives the exciting story of Elymas the Sorcerer who withstood Paul and sought to turn away the deputy from the faith. Paul said to him:

O full of all subtilty and all mischief, thou child of the devil, thou enemy of all righteousness, wilt thou not cease to pervert the right ways of the Lord?

And now, behold, the hand of the Lord is upon thee, and thou shalt be blind, not seeing the sun for a season. And immediately there fell on him a mist and a darkness; and he went about seeking some to lead him by the hand (vv. 10,11).

Through the discerning of spirits, Paul recognized that Elymas was a sorcerer, full of evil.

In Acts 19, there were vagabond Jews, who thought they could call out the name of Jesus over people and cause evil spirits to leave. They would say: *We adjure you by Jesus whom Paul preacheth* (v. 13). Paul knew and understood that these people were evil by the power of the Lord Jesus Christ.

The Gifts of Healing

The healing power of God flowed from this man, Paul. He demonstrated the gifts of healing in Acts 14:8-10: *And there sat a certain man at Lystra, impotent in his feet, being a cripple from his mother's womb, who never had walked* (v. 8). With a loud voice, Paul said to the man: *Stand upright on thy feet* (v. 10). Immediately, the man leaped and walked.

Paul's own testimony says: *I will not dare to speak of any of those things which Christ hath not wrought by me, to make the Gentiles obedient, by word and deed* (Rom. 15:18). The Gentiles, which includes all nations except the Jews, must be made obedient "by word and by deed." These must always go together. Paul goes on to explain why:

Through mighty signs and wonders, by the power of the Spirit of God; so that from Jerusalem, and round about Illyricum, I have fully preached the gospel of Christ.

Yea, so have I strived to preach the gospel, not where Christ was named, lest I should build upon another man's foundation (vv. 19,20).

Paul says without doubt that he saw signs and wonders in his ministry. He was bold to declare that he did not come second to Peter or any of the other disciples, but that he had the gifts of the Spirit flowing through him just as they had.

The Gift of Faith

We can see the gift of faith demonstrated through Paul in Acts, chapter 16, when Paul and Silas are in prison, hands and feet bound with iron. They had been beaten with stripes and the blood was running down their backs, itching and burning. There was no way they could help themselves. They could have cried and complained, but what did they do? The Bible says that at midnight they sang praises to God! (Acts 16:25.)

The gift of faith began to function! That old jail began to shake; their bonds dropped off; the doors were flung open; and that Philippian jailer fell to his knees, wanting to know what he could do to be saved. That same night the jailer and his whole house were saved and baptized. That's fast movement! And it all happened because of the faith that God had planted within their hearts.

Again, we see the gift of faith through Paul in Acts, chapter 28:

And when Paul had gathered a bundle of sticks, and laid them on the fire, there came a viper out of the heat, and fastened on his hand . . . And he shook off the beast into the fire, and felt no harm (vv. 3,5).

When the viper had attached itself to Paul's hand, he did not react in fear. He just shook it off into the fire. The faith flowing through him surged out and he "felt no harm."

The Working of Miracles

Two examples of the gift of the working of miracles through Paul can be seen in Acts 19 and 20. In Acts 19 there were miracles of healing: *And God wrought special miracles by the hands of Paul: so that from his body were brought unto the sick handkerchiefs or aprons, and the diseases departed from them, and the evil spirits went out of them* (vv. 11,12). Healing was an area in which Paul had full blessing. In Acts 20:7-12 Paul raised the dead:

And upon the first day of the week, when the disciples came together to break bread, Paul preached unto them, ready to depart on the morrow; and continued his speech until midnight. And there were many lights in the upper chamber, where they were gathered together.

And there sat in a window a certain young man name Eutychus, being fallen into a deep sleep: and as Paul was long preaching, he sunk down with sleep, and fell down from the third loft, and was taken up dead.

And Paul went down, and fell on him, and embracing him said, Trouble not yourselves; for his life is in him.

When he therefore was come up again, and had broken bread, and eaten, and talked a long while, even till break of day, so he departed. And they brought the young man alive, and were not a little comforted.

In this incident the word of knowledge also was demonstrated. Paul knew that life was in that young man, but he could not know it by looking at him or by feeling him. There was no physical evidence of life. Paul knew that life was in him because of the gift of the Holy Spirit.

The Gift of Prophecy

In 1 Corinthians 14:3 Paul speaks about the gift of prophecy: *He that prophesieth speaketh unto men to edification, and exhortation, and comfort.* These are the three vital categories of blessing within the gift of prophecy. Whenever a person prophesies in church, it should always accomplish at least one of these three blessings: to edify, or build up; to exhort, or encourage; and to comfort, or bring healing to the inner man.

The Apostle Paul possessed the gift of prophecy. It functioned through him to bless multitudes.

The Gift of Tongues

We know Paul possessed the gift of tongues because in 1 Corinthians 14:18 he wrote: *I thank my God, I speak with tongues more than ye all.* He goes on in the next verse to say: *Yet in the church I had rather speak five words with my understanding, that by my voice I might teach others also, than ten thousand words in an unknown tongue.*

The gift of tongues is the elementary gift — the first gift you receive. Tongues is the open door to the other gifts, the starting place, because it is communication with God. *He that speaketh in an unknown tongue edifieth himself* (1 Cor. 14:4). Through tongues, you edify yourself, or build up yourself on the inside. It is your spirit communicating directly with the Father in heaven.

The Interpretation of Tongues

Paul said many things about the gift of the interpretation of tongues. One thing that seems to be neglected by some church bodies is found in 1 Corinthians 14:27: *If any man speak in an unknown tongue, let it be by two, or at the most by three, and that by course; and let one interpret.* When one person gives forth a message in an unknown tongue, another should interpret. If the same person does both the speaking and the interpreting, he is limiting Jesus. The gift functions best when two people are involved rather than one.

Paul wrote: *Having then gifts differing according to the grace that is given to us, whether prophecy, let us prophesy according to the proportion of faith* (Rom. 12:6). Every gift of the Spirit functions by faith.

A Possessor of the Gifts

The Apostle Paul led the way in the gifts of the Spirit. He witnessed mighty deeds and glorious deliverances. In 1 Corinthians 7:7 he wrote: *For I would that all men were even as I myself. But every* man hath his proper gift of God, one after this manner, and another after that.

Not only did Paul teach us and present the broad scope of all these beautiful gifts, but he allowed them to function in his own life. We have merely touched upon them. An in-depth study of Paul's writings would reveal a wealth of information as to how the gifts functioned in his life and ministry.

I thank God that Paul was, not only a teacher, but a possessor, which is how we should wish to be. We should not be satisfied with being taught about the gifts of the Holy Spirit, but should want to possess them, so that in these last days the gifts pour forth through us in a mighty way.

13
How You Can Receive the Gifts

In order to receive things from God, you must first have knowledge. God cannot bless ignorance. Matthew's Gospel, chapter 4, describes Jesus' ministry: *And Jesus went about all Galilee, teaching in their synagogues, and preaching the gospel of the kingdom, and healing all manner of sickness and all manner of disease among the people* (v. 23). Jesus was first a teacher, then a preacher, then a healer.

Teaching is so important. Without it, there would be no depth of the Word to hold onto after salvation. If you teach a man about the Gospel, then give him the good news that he can have it, there will be something he can hold onto and the miracles will begin to flow.

In this final chapter on the gifts of the Spirit, I want to share how you personally can receive the gifts of the Holy Spirit. Definitions and identifications relating to the gifts of the Spirit are not sufficient. You must also know how you can receive these gifts in your own life.

Let me emphasize one point: If you are trying to drink water out of an empty well, you will get only dirt. If you are seeking your source of strength at a church that has no blessing in it, you will be unable to function in the gifts of the Holy Spirit. To function in the Spirit, you must go where the Spirit functions.

How can you receive the gifts of the Spirit? Here are some of the ways:

By receiving the promise.

On the day of Pentecost, Simon Peter said: *Repent, and be baptized every one of you in the name of Jesus for the remission of sins, and ye shall receive the gift of the Holy Ghost. For the promise is unto you, and to your children, and to all that are afar off, even as many as the Lord our God shall call* (Acts 2:38,39).

When God makes a promise, He keeps it. You can begin seeking the gifts of the Spirit because the Lord said you could have them. They are for you, for your children, and for *every* believer. The first way to receive the gifts of the Spirit in your life is by saying, "The promises are mine."

By divine revelation.

The Apostle Paul received the gifts of the Spirit through divine revelation from God. In Galatians 1:17,18 he wrote: *Neither went I up to Jerusalem to them which were apostles before me; but I went into Arabia, and returned again unto Damascus. Then after three years I went up to Jerusalem to see Peter, and abode with him fifteen days.* Paul went to Jerusalem to show Peter all the gifts and revelation he had received. No human being taught Paul; he was instructed by the Holy Spirit.

In Matthew 16:16 Peter said to Jesus: *Thou art the Christ, the Son of the living God.* Jesus answered with these words: *Blessed art thou, Simon Bar-jona: for flesh and blood hath not revealed it unto thee, but my Father which is in heaven* (v. 17). Peter did not learn this from any earthly source. The Father in heaven revealed it to him.

We can receive these gifts directly by revelation from God. I have met people in many countries who received the gifts of the Spirit, having never heard one word about them from any human. God can do things sovereignly.

By the laying on of hands.

Timothy received the gifts of the Spirit through the laying on of hands. We see this in 1 Timothy 4:14: *Neglect not the gift* (gift of the Holy Spirit), *which was given thee by prophecy, with the laying on of the hands of the presbytery.* Strong men of God — Paul, Barnabas, and Silas — laid their hands on Timothy and instantly the gifts of the Spirit began to function in this young man's life.

By desiring them.

There are several scriptures which show that you will not receive these gifts until you intelligently seek after them. They will not become a part of your life accidentally or casually.

Paul tells us to *covet earnestly the best gifts* and to *desire spiritual gifts* (1 Cor. 12:31; 14:1). The word *covet* is such a strong word. If you do not intensely desire these gifts and seek God with your total heart, you will never get them. The gifts of the Spirit are not delivered to complacent people. They are not rocking chair gifts; they are battlefront gifts. Spiritual power does not come easy. If you expect a great move of God in your life, you must consecrate yourself.

That desire for spiritual gifts must come from within you. It is a craving coming up out of you like liquid fire, so that you say with determination: *I will receive.*

Then in 1 Corinthians 14:12, Paul says: *Even so ye, forasmuch as ye are zealous of spiritual gifts,*

seek that ye may excel to the edifying of the church.
There are two words in this verse which need
special emphasis: *zealous* and *seek.* We are to be
zealous of spiritual gifts and *seek* to excel in them. To
seek a fortune requires effort. You have to go out
after it, not just sit in the house all day. To excel in
spiritual gifts, you have to keep moving. You cannot
receive the full manifestation of any gift of the Spirit
by stopping to rest on a spiritual plateau.

How I Received The Gifts

Witnessing the lives and ministries of men like
Howard Carter and Smith Wigglesworth stirred a
desire deep within me to be a part of God's move in
the earth. As I observed these men, both publicly and
privately, I experienced the kind of burning within
me that the disciples must have known while walking
with the Lord Jesus.

The gifts of the Spirit began to function through
me as I was a missionary on the foreign field. The
first gift to manifest was the discerning of spirits. I
was ministering for just one night in a Full Gospel
church in Java. During the service a little girl left her
seat and began to writhe like a snake. The pastor
and elders did not react, but within my spirit I heard
God say: "That is a devil." I had never before seen
anything like it — a human being so abused by the
Devil.

When I took the pulpit, I said to her, "Get up
and sit on that pew!" Though she did not understand
English and I could not speak her language, she
instantly returned to her seat. As I preached the
sermon, she just sat there, gazing up at me.

When I had finished my sermon, I leaned over and said, "Now come out of her!" Instantly she was delivered and the power of God hit that vast audience. Hundreds of people received salvation that night. Before I could give an invitation for them to get saved, they began streaming to the altar to give their hearts to God.

14
The Devil's Counterfeit

One thing we must guard against spiritually is the Devil's counterfeiting of these supernatural gifts of the Holy Spirit. Satan is a deceiver. The Bible says he sometimes appears as an angel of light — a counterfeit angel. (2 Cor. 11:14.) There will even be a counterfeit Christ called the Antichrist. In all of history, anything that was of value has almost invariably had some form of counterfeit. Naturally, then, we can expect the Devil to counterfeit the nine gifts of the Spirit.

Some people cannot see the real for the counterfeit, but I believe the Spirit of God within us will reveal to us whether or not something is real. No one should ever be confused about what is real and what is counterfeit. God wants us to know these things.

The Word of Wisdom

The gift of the word of God's wisdom is the ability to know and understand about future events. Every great prophet of the Old and New Testaments functioned in this gift, and today there are men and women who supernaturally know things that are to come to pass. We sincerely feel that we have come to that place in history when this gift is going to be tremendously increased, whether it is called the prophetic ministry or the gift of the word of wisdom.

God has always wanted to show His people the future. He sent an angel to inform Abraham in advance that He was going to destroy the cities of Sodom and Gomorrah because of their terrible wickedness. God does not want to hide from us the things He is going to do.

In 1 Corinthians 12:8-10 God gives us an outline of the true gifts of the Holy Spirit: *For to one is given by the Spirit the word of wisdom.*

Has the Devil sought to counterfeit the word of wisdom? Yes, and not just from the beginning of the Church, but from the beginning of time. These counterfeits are called witches.

A witch is a person who seeks to know from supernatural sources other than God things not known normally or naturally. Their supernatural source is the Devil. No wonder the Bible says in many places that the land should be free of witches. Why? Because they try to assume the place of God. They lead people to worship the wrong entity. You cannot worship both the Living God and the Devil at the same time.

Anyone who follows the satanic counterfeits of the gifts of the Spirit will never see heaven or God. We oppose these counterfeiters, not only because they are worthless, but because they lead to destruction. If one is going to dabble in the occult to try to know the future, he will only know damnation and sorrow. He will not find that which his heart desires. He will not know truth, only deception.

The Devil has no relationship with truth. Jesus said of the Devil: *... there is no truth in him ... for he is a liar, and the father of it* (John 8:44). He was a liar from the beginning, and he always will be. If you believe him, you will be deceived.

Witches, soothsayers, and magicians seek to know the future and the unknown by satanic powers.

God says we should not be part of these people. In 2 Corinthians 11:13 such are called *false apostles, deceitful workers, transforming themselves into the apostles of Christ.* Verse 14 says: *Satan himself is transformed into an angel of light.* It is no marvel then that his ministers are also tranformed into false ministers of righteousness, *whose end shall be according to their works* (v. 15).

Above all, God wants us to live in truth. If there is a problem ahead, we need to know about it. Whether it is a problem in our ministry, our home, or our church, we need to be aware so we can deal with it. God wants us to know.

Some ministers say, "Don't talk about the Devil. You are eulogizing him." Closing our eyes to Satan and his devices does not take them away. Whenever I talk about the Devil, he is not eulogized. He is greatly offended, greatly hurt, and greatly defeated!

The Devil does have counterfeits, and the Word of God warns us that they pose as apostles and prophets. We must be on guard against them. How can we recognize such people? You will know every man by his fruits. (Matt. 12:33.) You will know every person by the spirit that is within him. God will reveal these things to us through prayer and listening to His still, small voice as the Spirit speaks to us.

I must say emphatically regarding the word of wisdom that if anyone stands and offers himself as a prophet of God to tell you the future, just check one thing: Does it come to pass? If it does not, then he is to be branded for what he is: a false prophet. He should be put out of the Church. The Church of Jesus Christ is no place for humbug!

In our church fellowship we permit no foolishness within the Body of the Lord Jesus Christ. If anyone wishes to prophesy about the future, we say, "Go ahead, but it had better come to pass!" We permit no false prophets to function in our midst. God knows what He is doing; and if someone says something that is wrong, then we have no need to hear from him again. We want to hear from the Holy Ghost. We want the gifts of the Spirit to function, but they can function only through the Body of Christ — holy and pure and clean.

God's people do not need witches or soothsayers or magicians to know what God is going to do in the future. I feel very sorry for people who always want to know what is going to happen tomorrow. What is going to happen, will happen. Why should we worry? If we walk with Jesus, it is going to be good! All you have to do is to live for Him — love Him and serve Him — and everything will be good! If you are going to walk by faith, let Him hold the future. Just say: "Lord Jesus, You hold the future, so I know it will be good. I'm satisfied."

The Word of Knowledge

The second of the gifts of the Spirit that the Devil would love to counterfeit is the gift of the word of God's knowledge. While the word of wisdom concerns the future, the word of knowledge deals with that which already exists. Knowledge is a fact — something that exists now, not in the future.

The word of knowledge is that gift given by God which allows a person to know something he cannot learn through his natural senses. God reveals it to his spirit. The Devil, of course, would love to have people do that, too; only he uses false knowledge. The Devil will "reveal" things, but his purpose is to trick you, to deceive you, to lead you into a trap.

There are people who go to palm readers and mediums seeking knowledge supernaturally. Sometimes when a person has lost something, he will consult a medium to find out where the lost article is. If you do this, I have just one thing to tell you: It will follow you home and eventually cause you grief, because you are dealing with an evil spirit.

If you go to a seance and become involved in the occult, you open yourself to satanic influence. Whenever you become involved in this type of activity — in these things which belong to Satan — it is not just a onetime deal. You are entering into a relationship that could carry you right to your grave. This is dangerous business!

You have to recognize that you have an enemy. The Devil will do all in his power to rob you of the use of the spiritual gifts which you possess, because without the gifts functioning in the Church, we cannot win the battle of these last days.

Once a couple had planned to fly to one of our meetings to bring their mentally afflicted son for healing. These parents later told us that, though they had not even told the boy about it, the night before they were to leave, he ran away. He was acting on knowledge that the Devil had put in him. The parents had made preparations to bring the boy for deliverance from that demon within him, and the demon tried to interfere.

There are thousands of people who need to be set free, just like this boy, but the Devil is keeping them in bondage. He does not want God's people to have the power and authority to set others free. But this is a glorious hour, a victory hour. We must press hard to identify the Devil and his schemes to counterfeit God's great and precious gifts.

Discerning of Spirits

There is a great attempt in our country today to "get inside" people through some potentially dangerous forms of psychology and psychiatry. ESP is terribly dangerous. If you try to reach beyond the human mind to gain information supernaturally, the only force you will contact is the Devil. God cannot be reached through this type of manifestation.

In our world today we have mind readers and gurus with all sorts of philosophies. We have people who are trained to discern the inner man; but all of it is a counterfeit, belonging only to the Devil. It has no relationship to reality and God does not want us to take part in such things.

The mind is a very precious commodity. Be careful not to loan it to a stranger. Give it only to Jesus.

The Gift of Faith

I can assure you that the Devil would love to simulate this precious gift. The gift of faith is a remarkable gift. There is no human energy exercised in this gift; it comes purely from the power of God flowing through a person.

The Devil would have us to believe that the things we desire will come simply by believing for

182

them — which is a form of witchcraft. In fact, curses come about this way, especially in places where black magic is a common practice. In Indonesia if a woman wanted to destroy her husband, she could pay a visit to the witch doctor. He would take a little doll, which represents the husband, start putting pins into it, and say incantations. The husband is supposed to get sick and die. They claim that it works — that he would die without their touching him.

If we were talking about the things of God, we would call that an instrument of faith — believing something to happen.

The Working of Miracles

Once while in Java we went to a village in which everyone, including the mayor, was a Christian. We found that it was a city of refuge. If a person was persecuted in some other village, he could go there to live in peace and security. In fact, most of the people living there were refugees who had come seeking escape from persecution.

It had all begun with a Dutch girl, who very innocently had gone to this place to preach. After a few days of listening to her preach, the witch doctor came to her and told her to leave. When she refused to go, he explained why he wanted her out of the village. He said, "I am the witch doctor here, and I was here first. It is not proper for two of us to be in the same territory."

The girl told him, "No, I'm not leaving. And I'm not into witchcraft as you are. I serve the Living God Who is in heaven above."

"I know nothing about that," the man answered. "I have heard you talking about miracles, and I am in charge of such things here. That is my job, so you will have to go!''

When the young lady refused, the witch doctor challenged her to a public contest with the understanding that the loser must pack up and leave. The girl agreed, not really knowing what she was getting into.

A public contest between the two was set to take place three days later. The girl did not know that the witch doctor was planning to spend those three days in fasting and prayer to the Devil, which he did. She went about her usual business without much thought of what she was facing.

They met together for the contest on a platform before the whole village: the witch doctor vs. the lady missionary. The witch doctor announced to the crowd that they were about to have a showdown to decide who was to stay and who was to leave. The village would belong to the strongest power.

The girl agreed, still not really knowing what the witch doctor had in mind.

He asked her, "Do you want to go first?"

"No," she answered, "you go ahead." That was a mistake.

He lay down on the wood floor and within one minute his whole body became as stiff as death. Then it gravitated, floating about ankle high. When it reached knee high, it just rested there. His eyes were closed; his body was straight as a board.

Needless to say, the girl was scared! There she was — a simple missionary girl, talking about Jesus — and here was a witch doctor, floating knee high from the ground. She thought, "Well, Lord, it looks as if I may be leaving town."

As she was standing there dumbfounded, looking at the man, she prayed, "Lord, what shall I do? I came here to preach."

The Lord answered, "Get him down."

"But, Lord, how can I do that?"

"Knock him down."

"Lord, how should I knock him down?"

"Put your foot on him."

So that little woman walked over to the floating witch doctor, placed her foot on his stomach, and pushed him to the floor. Then the Lord said, "Tell that unclean spirit to come out."

She screamed, "Come out of him, you unclean spirit!"

The witch doctor went into a convulsion, then woke up. The first thing he said was, "Where am I?" He had become so full of the Devil that he had no idea where he was or how he got there.

The missionary said to him, "All these people came to see who was the most powerful. Now, are you ready to receive Jesus as Lord?"

"Yes," he answered. She led him in the sinner's prayer and he gave his heart to Jesus. Then she asked him, "Do you want the Holy Ghost?"

He said, "I want everything you have." She laid hands on him and he received the infilling of the Holy Ghost right there before that group of people.

After the meeting he said, "I don't want you to leave," so she said, "All right. Let's have our own city."

He told her, "You be the top administrator and I
will be the mayor." Together they chose the rest of
the organization for the city. Our party stayed there
for several days, and it was one of the happiest
communities I have ever seen.

That witch doctor had the power to float, but it
was not God's power. It was a counterfeit, and God's
power superceded it.

We see the same in Exodus, chapter 7, when
Moses and Aaron stood before the Pharaoh of Egypt.
Pharaoh demanded Moses to show him a miracle, so
Aaron threw down his rod and it became a serpent.
Immediately, Pharaoh called his sorcerers and they
did the same thing. They threw down their rods, and
they also became snakes, . . . *but Aaron's rod
swallowed up their rods* (v. 12).

There will be times of contests like this for the
Church. We must know what is spiritual. If we do
not, the Devil will defeat us. There are thousands of
people in our country today who have been deceived
by the Devil's power. But as God's people, we must
not be among those who have been deceived.

The Gifts of Healing

This may be the biggest counterfeit of all.
Healing cults have existed almost from the beginning
of time. Recently my wife was telling me about a cult
in the Philippines that performs surgery without a
knife, with just their fingers. Swarms of people from
England, Canada, Australia, the United States, and
Sweden were traveling to the Philippines for this
"miracle healing." I knew about it when we lived
there in the Philippines, but no one was coming then.

Now literally thousands of people have been deceived by it.

I know of a doctor there whose brother claimed to have experienced one of those "miracle surgeries." He claimed that his gallstones had been removed without an incision, without leaving a scar. When the doctor persuaded his brother to be examined, the X rays clearly showed that the gallstones were still there. Not only had the man been deceived about his health, he had also been cheated out of the money he had spent for his "miracle."

Some people think that when they are "healed," it is only temporary. Healing cults will say things like that. But that is only the Devil. When God heals, it is permanent!

I was healed of tuberculosis by God's power. At the time nobody was praying for me. No one was in the room except my parents and me. I had a tubercular fever and was spitting up blood. The doctor said I would die that night, but God healed me. There was no "hocus-pocus" and no burning of incense.

God's healings are always clean, pure, and above reproach, undeniable. The Devil's "healings" are always mystical and shrouded in a cloud.

The Gift of Prophecy

And when they (Paul and Barnabas) had gone through the isle unto Paphos, they found a certain sorcerer, a false prophet, a Jew, whose name was Bar-jesus: which was with the deputy of the country, Sergius Paulus, a prudent man; who called for

187

Barnabas and Saul, and desired to hear the word of God.

But Elymas the sorcerer (for so is his name by interpretation) withstood them, seeking to turn away the deputy from the faith.

Then Saul, (who also is called Paul), filled with the Holy Ghost, set his eyes on him,

And said, O full of all subtilty and all mischief, thou child of the devil, thou enemy of all righteousness, wilt thou not cease to pervert the right ways of the Lord?

And now, behold, the hand of the Lord is upon thee, and thou shalt be blind, not seeing the sun for a season. And immediately there fell on him a mist and a darkness; and he went about seeking some to lead him by the hand.

Then the deputy, when he saw what was done, believed, being astonished at the doctrine of the Lord.

Acts 13:6-12

I feel from the depths of my spirit that there are going to be people just like this man Elymas — deceivers, deceiving government leaders. Washington is full of them. There are more people in Washington practicing black magic and divination than probably any other city in America. In the city of Philadelphia there are 3,000 registered witches.

We are living in the last days, and in these last days God wants to pour out His Spirit upon all flesh. You and I are those receivers of God's power, just like the Apostle Paul. We are to rebuke that which is evil and to keep our nation clean by the power of God. There is no other way for this nation to stay clean spiritually except by the power of God working through His Church — and it will work today as it worked in the early Church.

Speaking In Tongues

Another of these counterfeits of Satan may seem strange to us, but I believe the Devil seeks to counterfeit the gift of speaking in tongues. I have seen dozens and dozens of people uttering things that could not be understood either by the other native people in the meeting or by me as a foreign visitor. They were merely stammering out words under demonic power.

Anything that God does — no matter what it is — the Devil will try to counterfeit. We, as the children of the Most High God, must learn to recognize these counterfeits. We are to stand in the truth always, and to stand strong. If we do, God will give us the victory. No devil in hell — no evil, no lie, no counterfeit — can stand against us.

If we stand in truth, we also stand in power, knowing that we will win every time. God did not send us out into the world unequipped for the job. We are to invade the devil's territory, tear him to pieces, and destroy him, as well as any manifestation he has on the gifts of the Holy Spirit.

In the high mountains of Luzon in the Philippines, among very primitive people, I built a little church of metal and concrete blocks. I went there to dedicate this little church without knowing that the chief witch in the area had said she would come and close the meeting. I knew nothing about it, nor did any of the members of that congregation.

Just as I started to speak, a woman in the back stood up and began to say unintelligible words. Later the people said they had never heard anything like it and had no idea what she was saying. Since I was a foreigner, I did not know if she was speaking the native language of the people, but inside I knew something was wrong. My spirit knew it was a demonic manifestation. So I leaned over and said to her, "Shut up and sit down!" And she did!

God gave us a great meeting that night. Many people were saved. News spread the next day that the woman still was unable to speak. God had locked her jaws!

When I commanded her, in Jesus' name, to shut up and sit down, fear came upon those heathen people and they thought, "We had better serve the Living God and leave this witchcraft alone."

This will happen. If we will speak the truth and resist evil, many people will be brought to God.

The Devil will try to counterfeit the gifts of tongues and interpretation of tongues, so we must be on guard against his deceptions.

The Antichrist

Now let's look at a very important type of deception — the Antichrist, who will come upon the face of the earth and deceive the world through counterfeit gifts of the Spirit.

Revelation 13:15 says that the False Prophet will have power to give life unto the image of the Beast (the Antichrist). This same chapter speaks of three spirits who came out of the river. One of them entered into the dragon, that is the Devil.

There are going to be *three demonic deceptions* in the last days:

First, there will be *a moral deception.* Satan's deception from the Garden of Eden until now has never changed; it is a moral deception. Look how he deceived Eve and how he tried to deceive Jesus. He will be doing the same thing in these last days. He has not learned one new thing in these 6,000 years. He is still doing the same thing in the same way; there have been no alterations, no changes.

Secondly, there will be *a political deception.* I assure you that in the near future there will be politicians on the world scene who will speak words so amazing that the world will follow them. They will have promises so astounding that the whole world will say, "Let's follow after this person." This is the spirit of antichrist.

Thirdly, there will be *a religious deception.* This will be the False Prophet, which is the religious spirit.

The Devil will deceive by miracles. Revelation 13:14 states that he *deceiveth them that dwell on the earth by the means of those miracles which he had power to do in the sight of the beast . . . .* These miracles will be performed in the sight of the man who is the Antichrist, just as the Egyptian sorcerers had the power to do false miracles in the eyes of Pharaoh. But Moses put an end to all of that. What a sinner sees and what God's servant sees are two entirely different things. They may believe a lie, but we will not.

The Devil will deceive people, . . . *saying to them that dwell on the earth, that they should make*

191

an image to the beast, which had the wound by a sword, and did live (v. 14). Here we see the healing of a deadly wound, so that the people believe that he is God. There are many false healers making the rounds today, deceiving many.

I beheld another beast coming up out of the earth; and he had two horns like a lamb (this is the False Prophet), *and he spake as a dragon.*

And he exerciseth all the power of the first beast before him (the Antichrist), *whose deadly wound was healed.*

Revelation 13:11,12

So we find that this beast could do things which to the people were completely supernatural. We know these things are not honest and true; they are counterfeit. But the Bible says the whole world will go after it. Jesus said: *I am come in my Father's name, and ye receive me not: if another shall come in his own name, him ye will receive* (John 5:43).

We live in a strange world today. There are people who will pass up the truth in order to grab a lie. This world would love to have the benefit and blessing of healing without having to get right with God. Then they could go on living in sin and still get their miracle free of charge. But that is not how it works. Jesus told the man who had been healed at the Pool of Bethesda: *Behold, thou art made whole: sin no more, lest a worse thing come unto thee* (John 5:14).

Revelation 13:13 says: *And he doeth great wonders, so that he maketh fire come down from heaven on the earth in the sight of men.* Notice that this deception is done *in the sight of men*. It is a magician's trick, a counterfeit.

The Bible tells us that when the Antichrist comes, it will be through a great system of deception; so it is obvious that the way before him will already be prepared. When he comes, it will be easy because the people will already be conditioned for him.

Today our world is conditioned for a lie. Almost every television program you see shows a superman. The Antichrist will be that superman, and this gullible world will say, "Who is like him? We must all follow him."

The climax of it all will be the Antichrist, in whom a counterfeit of all nine gifts will be manifested. They who have refused the gifts from us will accept the counterfeit gifts from him. Isn't that sorrowful? Tens of thousands of people who do not accept healing from the stripes of the Lord Jesus Christ will accept it from spiritism, or from some pseudo-science that has no blood sacrifice attached to it.

I urge you to commit yourself to stand against the counterfeits that Satan will bring into the world. Say: "God, I am against these counterfeits of Satan, and I am going to fight them. I will recognize them when they rise up, expose them for what they are, and resist them, in Jesus' name. I will be on Jesus' side every time."

Part II
Ministries of the
Holy Spirit

Introduction

In addition to the nine separate and distinct gifts of the Holy Spirit, there are nine offices of ministry that were given to the Church after the resurrection of the Lord Jesus Christ. We could call them "resurrection gifts," because they were given to the Body of Christ after the Resurrection and will belong to us until the Lord Jesus returns for His Church. In the book of Ephesians, chapter 4, we read about these nine ministry gifts.

But unto every one of us is given grace, (that is our salvation) according to the measure of the gift of Christ.

Ephesians 4:7

We are given the gift of God according to the measure of the gift of Christ. Christ freely and abundantly gave His total life, reserving nothing; so we receive, in like manner, the gifts of God — in fullness and total capacity. God is not stingy with His giving. He gives abundantly, so we should receive abundantly.

Wherefore he saith, When he (Christ) ascended up on high, he led captivity captive, and gave gifts unto men.

Ephesians 4:8

The Lord Jesus Christ, through the instrument of the Holy Spirit, gives two types of gifts:

1. the gifts of the Holy Ghost — the nine gifts of the Spirit.

2. men and women as gifts to the Body.

These "gifts to the Body" are listed in verse 11: *And he gave some, apostles; and some, prophets; and some, evangelists; and some, pastors and teachers.*

In 1 Corinthians 12:28 we find two other groups — *helps* and *governments* — and in 1 Timothy 3 are mentioned the offices of *bishop*, or *elder*, and *deacon*.

We will examine each of these nine ministries further in our study, but first let's consider the ninefold purpose of these ministries.

15
Ninefold Purpose of Ministry Gifts

God never gives anything without a purpose. In Ephesians 4:12-16 after listing the five major ministry gifts to the Body of Christ, the Apostle Paul states the ninefold purpose of these ministries to the Church:

For the perfecting of the saints, for the work of the ministry, for the edifying of the body of Christ:

Till we all come in the unity of the faith, and of the knowledge of the Son of God, unto a perfect man, unto the measure of the stature of the fulness of Christ:

That we henceforth be no more children, tossed to and fro, and carried about with every wind of doctrine, by the sleight of men, and cunning craftiness, whereby they lie in wait to deceive;

But speaking the truth in love, may grow up into him in all things, which is the head, even Christ:

From whom the whole body fitly joined together and compacted by that which every joint supplieth, according to the effectual working in the measure of every part, maketh increase of the body unto the edifying of itself in love.

1. For the perfecting of the saints.

When God calls an apostle, a prophet, an evangelist, a pastor, or a teacher, it is for one purpose: the perfecting of the saints. This person is to give himself. No gift that God gives is ever for self. When we say, "Lord, bless me," God can't hear that prayer. He wants us to bless others. When He gives us something, it is to share with someone else.

A little boy handed his lunch of fish and bread to the Lord Jesus and said, "This is all I have," then he stood back to see what would happen. The Lord Jesus began to break it and hand it to His disciples — not for them to eat or to shove into their pockets for tomorrow's lunch, but for them to pass out to others.

When Jesus handed out the bread and fish to His disciples, it was for one purpose: to meet people's needs. It is not God's purpose just to enrich us, but to make us into people who can enrich others. If we fail to share our gifts with others, these gifts will soon fade away.

Christianity is a unique institution. If we take it and put it in a golden box, it will die. Christianity does not fit in a box. It was made for only one purpose: to be given to the world — to all those in the highways and byways, the fugitives, the outcasts, both the down-and-outers and the up-and-outers. If you take the Gospel of Christ and keep it inside the four walls of a church, it will perish. It was made to be shared — to be spread to all those people outside the church who have never met the Lord Jesus. And so it is with these ministries: they were created for action. If you are given one of these ministries, it is to be used, first of all, to perfect the saints.

2. For the work of the ministry.

The ministry of the Lord Jesus Christ requires work. There is much work to be done — apostolic, prophetic, evangelistic, pastoral, and teaching work of the ministry. Laborers are needed in the fields to bring in the harvest.

3. For the edifying of the Body of Christ.

These ministry gifts are for the edifying, or building up, of the Body of Christ. None of them has to do with inward and selfish motives. Each has to do with the life of Jesus pouring out of those who possess them — giving of ourselves, blessing others and helping others. The whole structure of Christianity is built upon the concept of blessing others. That is what Jesus and the salvation message are all about.

4. Till we all come in the unity of the faith . . .

It hurts to see Christians divided one against the other, denomination against denomination. If all the churches in America were to suddenly start working together, the Devil would have to pack up and leave this country! But as long as we are divided and fighting against each other, he has the advantage over us. He will lose that advantage when we all come into the unity of the faith.

5. . . . and of the knowledge of the Son of God . . .

It is easy to have knowledge about so many things except Jesus. We are to come into a true knowledge of the Son of God — who He is, what He is, what He has done, and what He can do. What a tremendous thing it will be when all of us really and truly know the totality of what Jesus Christ can do for us. He is not a has-been God; He is the Living God. Anything He has ever done, He can still do! Anything He *can* do, He *will* do!

6. . . . unto a perfect man . . .

God is shooting for high stakes. He is not looking for imperfection; He is not looking for defeat. He intends to have these ministries and gifts in the Body of Christ until we become a perfect man!

7. . . . unto the measure of the stature of the fulness of Christ . . .

What a magnificent thing! We are going to keep these ministries active until we bring the total Body *unto the measure of the stature of the fulness of Christ.* Look at Christ standing tall — with faith, with no fear of any kind — before demons, demoniacs, and raging storms. It didn't matter! There was no fear! We are to bring our people up to that same measure — as tall and strong and confident as Jesus Christ. That is our goal.

8. . . . That we henceforth be no more children . . .

It amazes me sometimes how a person can be a Christian for years and still act like they are about three months old, screaming about everything that doesn't suit them. God says that henceforth we are to *be no more children, tossed to and fro, and carried about with every wind of doctrine, by the sleight of men.* Some people will believe anything they hear, but we are to stick to the great principles of divine truth in the Word of God. This is one of the functions of the ministry gifts: to instruct us and to keep us from being led astray into false doctrines by deceitful men.

9. . . . But speaking the truth in love . . .

Now to me it is a great commission to speak the truth in love. We are to speak God's truth not in anger, but only in love. Why? That all of us might grow up in Christ:

. . . Speaking the truth in love, (you) may grow up into him in all things, which is the head, even Christ:

From whom the whole body fitly joined together and compacted by that which every joint supplieth, according to the effectual working in the measure of every part, maketh increase of the body unto the edifying of itself in love.

The Lord Jesus Christ is the Head; and from Him, the whole Body is fitly joined together. You are what you are — and what you are going to be — because Christ has joined you there. Don't worry about what you will be. He will get you there; He never fails.

We are fitly joined together as a body by Him; and we are compacted together in strength, so that every joint — each of us — is a part of the Body.

This is the ninefold purpose of the ministry gifts which are given unto the Body of the Lord Jesus Christ. Now we will view each gift individually in the light of God's Word.

16
The Fivefold Ministry Gifts

And he gave some, apostles; and some, prophets; and some, evangelists; and some, pastors and teachers; for the perfecting of the saints, for the work of the ministry, for the edifying of the body of Christ.

Ephesians 4:11

The Office of Apostle

The first position of church leadership we will give attention to is the office of apostle. There are those who say there are no more apostles in the world — that all the apostles died out with the original twelve — but as we will see, apostleship was not confined to the original twelve disciples. There are at least twenty-four apostles mentioned in the New Testament alone, and I believe there are apostles in the Church today. As long as there is a Church, there will be apostles.

I know men today with apostolic ministries — men around the world who are doing the work of an apostle at this very moment — and I believe there will be many more. In these last days the greatest ministries are going to become tremendously accelerated, along with the operation and functions of the Holy Spirit.

The office of apostle is the foremost ministry in the Church of the Lord Jesus Christ. An apostle is not appointed by men. The Bible says the Holy Ghost is the One Who establishes these ministries in the Church.

Let's look at the word *apostle*. There are several translations in the New Testament of the Greek word referring to the apostles. One of these translations is *apostolos*, meaning "a delegate; one sent with full power of attorney to act for another." An apostle is a divine delegate — one who has come to the people of the world, representing the Trinity in heaven. The apostle does not act in his own behalf; he is anointed by the Holy Spirit to act in behalf of the Body of Christ, the Church of the Lord Jesus Christ. In other words, an apostle is one delegated with the power of attorney to act in behalf of the Lord Jesus Christ, sent by the power of the Holy Ghost to you.

This word *apostolos* appears many times in the New Testament. It is translated *messenger* twice:

Whether any do inquire of Titus, he is my partner and fellowhelper concerning you: or our brethren be inquired of, they are the messengers of the churches, and the glory of Christ.

2 Corinthians 8:23

Yet I supposed it necessary to send to you Epaphroditus, my brother, and my companion in labour, and fellowsoldier, but your messenger . . . .

Philippians 2:25

Seventy-eight times the word *apostle* means "sent one." In John 13:16 Jesus said: *Verily, verily, I say unto you, The servant is not greater than his lord; neither he that is sent greater than he that sent him.* When an apostle goes forth, he is not greater than the One Who sent him; he is a representative of the One Who sent him. In other words, an apostle is one with delegated authority. He does not act on his own and do as he pleases; he is one sent forth from God with a message from God for the people. Now, that is a humbling situation.

The position of apostle, as the very word implies, means a person who is sent forth to do a work for God. Such a person is not greater than his Lord, not greater than the One Who sent him. The Lord Jesus Christ is always the Great One.

When an apostle comes into our midst, he is a gift of the Holy Ghost to us as a person. He did not become an apostle by studying or working hard; apostleship does not come that way. He was made an apostle by God. Apostles are born through the power of the Holy Ghost.

The apostle is different from the other four offices in that he has the ability to perform those other functions. This is what makes an apostle and why the Bible always lists the apostle first. Some people think the prophet should be first, but the apostle is above the prophet. Any person — man or woman — with an apostolic calling has the ability, the authority, and the anointing to raise up a church without any outside help. Paul had this amazing ability. He could enter a town, walk into the marketplace, and have a church formed before nightfall. He could stir up the Devil and divide a city within only a few hours. Not only could he raise up a church — establish it and found it — but he also had the power and ability to remain there as pastor. He could teach the people in that church, then start a school and send out workers to other places.

The apostle is a combination of the other four church ministries. He can be whatever is needed — pastor, evangelist, teacher, or prophet. In addition, the apostle can set church government in order. He can establish deacon boards and elderships, develop the ministry of helps within a church body, and place governments in a church so the body will function properly.

People today seem so reluctant to recognize the ministry of an apostle. We have no problem with the offices of pastor and evangelist, but we are almost afraid to call a man an apostle. We fear that pride could enter in and cause that person to be lifted up. But if a person is truly an apostle, he will never be prideful. When Moses' face shown with the glory of God, he was the last to realize it. A person with the true power of God oftentimes hardly recognizes it himself.

As long as we realize these gifts and ministerial abilities as spiritual qualities that God has placed within us, then there is no need for pride. If it is a gift of God, what do we have to be proud of? We did nothing to earn it; it was a gift from God.

If a minister fills all five offices of ministry to the Body of Christ, then he is an apostle.

New Testament Apostles

As mentioned above, there are at least twenty-four apostles listed in the New Testament. Let's examine some of them. You may be surprised at the first one: **the Lord Jesus Christ.** Hebrews 3:1 says:

Wherefore, holy brethren, partakers of the heavenly calling, consider the Apostle and High Priest of our profession, Christ Jesus.

Heaven sent Jesus: *God so loved the world, that he gave* (sent, delegated) *his only begotten Son* (the Lord Jesus Christ) . . . (John 3:16).

It is not difficult to understand that the Lord Jesus Christ was an apostle. The office of apostle involves the total ministry of God, and Christ had a total ministry. He was perhaps the only full-fledged, complete apostle the world has ever known — the total embodiment of what it means to be a "sent one" — delegated, as He often said, to do what He was told to do.

The Apostle Paul. In Galatians 1:1 we read:

Paul, an apostle (not of men, neither by man, but by Jesus Christ, and God the Father, who raised him from the dead).

Here Paul is defining apostleship and his relationship with the Body, which you can either accept or reject. If Paul was appointed to this job by the Holy Spirit, he is speaking by the anointing of the Holy Spirit and what he says must be totally true. He is saying, "I am Paul, an apostle."

If a person has a ministry ability, he should not hide it. It is nothing to be ashamed of. Paul was not hesitant at all about speaking of his relationship with God and of his calling by God. He says boldly: "I am an apostle (not of men, neither by man, but by Jesus Christ, and God the Father, who raised him from the dead)."

Then a little further in Galatians we read what Paul wrote about Peter: *For he that wrought effectually in Peter to the apostleship of the circumcision, the same was mighty in me toward the Gentiles* (Gal. 2:8). Paul was showing how Peter had become an apostle to a certain group, the circumcision (the Jews).

I have seen this demonstrated many times. Great men of God had tremendously effective ministries in one area or to one group of people, but they failed when attempting to minister in other places or to other groups. An apostle of God has an ability and a ministry, but he must be directed where God wants him. Not only does God have the right to make you something, He also has the right to tell you *where* to function. And if you think it will work wherever you please, just try it!

The First Twelve. Matthew 10:2-4 lists the first twelve apostles who walked with Jesus:

Now the names of the twelve apostles are these; The first, Simon, who is called Peter, and Andrew his brother; James the son of Zebedee, and John his brother; Philip, and Bartholomew; Thomas, and Matthew the publican; James the son of Alphaeus, and Lebbaeus, whose surname was Thaddaeus; Simon the Canaanite, and Judas Iscariot, who also betrayed him.

Jesus chose these men, set them aside, and anointed them — that they might be "sent ones," the cornerstones of the Church. These men were "super persons." Almost all of them died a martyr's death, giving their blood for the Church.

Matthias. After Judas betrayed the Lord Jesus and killed himself, the remaining eleven decided to choose another to take his place. We read in Acts 1:26:

And they gave forth their lots; and the lot fell upon Matthias; and he was numbered with the eleven apostles.

Barnabas. In 1 Corinthians 9:5,6 we read:

Have we not power to lead about a sister, a wife, as well as other apostles, and as the brethren of the Lord, and Cephas? Or I only and Barnabas, have not we power to forbear working?

Here Paul specifically states that Barnabas bore all the marks of apostleship, that he possessed all the abilities and ministries of apostleship. As far as Paul could determine, Barnabas was one of God's "sent ones."

Then there are some names that we know very little about:

Andronicus and Junia. In Romans 16:7 Paul writes:

Salute Andronicus and Junia, my kinsmen, and my fellowprisoners, who are of note among the apostles, who also were in Christ before me.

Paul was not the first person in his family to find Christ. He may have been fighting against his own family, even putting some of them in jail. He says here that his own kinsmen — Andronicus and Junia — were in Christ before he was, and that they were *of note among the apostles.*

Apollos. First Corinthians 4:6,9 says:

And these things, brethren, I have in a figure transferred to myself and to Apollos for your sakes; that ye might learn in us not to think of men above that which is written . . . For I think that God hath set forth us the apostles last . . . .

Paul clearly states here that Apollos was an apostle.

James, the Lord's brother. Galatians 1:19 says:

But other of the apostles saw I none, save James the Lord's brother.

James 1:1 reads:

James, a servant of God and of the Lord Jesus Christ, to the twelve tribes which are scattered abroad, greeting.

Silas and Timothy. In 1 Thessalonians 1:1 Paul begins his letter:

Paul, and Silvanus (Silas), and Timotheus (Timothy), unto the church of the Thessalonians.

In 1 Thessalonians 2:6 he writes:

Nor of men sought we glory, neither of you, nor yet of others, when we might have been burdensome, as the apostles of Christ.

We see here that Paul refers to Silas and Timothy as apostles of the Lord Jesus Christ.

Titus. In 2 Corinthians 8:23 we read:

Whether any do inquire of Titus, he is my partner and fellowhelper concerning you: or our brethren be inquired of, they are the messengers ("apostolos") of the churches, and the glory of Christ.

Here we see that Titus was an apostle, or a "sent one."

Epaphroditus. Philippians 2:25 says:

Yet I supposed it necessary to send to you Epaphroditus, my brother, and companion in labour, and fellowsoldier, but your messenger ("apostolos"), and he that ministered to my wants.

So we find in the New Testament that there were not just twelve apostles, nor did this office of ministry cease to exist when those twelve were gone from the earth.

The seventy that Jesus sent out were also men with an apostolic ministry. They were a follow-up

212

group, who ministered the same as the original twelve. (Luke 10:1.)

Ministry of An Apostle

Apostleship is a ministry for the Church as long as the Church is upon the face of this earth. They are the divine leaders God has commissioned to lead His Church.

An apostle is one who can pioneer, who can construct and begin a work with no problem. But not only can he conceive and bring into being a body of believers, he can remain behind to found that church and put it on a solid rock of truth. He can organize it, set it in order, and teach it with great fluency and accuracy.

A Price To Pay

All those who have a place of leadership in Christ Jesus will suffer persecution. The bigger the job, the dirtier the Devil wants to get you. But don't let that deter you. If you want leadership, reach for it. In Jesus' name, be what God wants you to be!

As a young man, I decided strongly that I would never permit the joy which had grown in my heart to be dependent on other people's opinions. If one person says I am great while another says I am nothing, neither of them affect me. Other people's opinions are no basis for our security; our security is in Jesus Christ. We are what we are by the power of God — and no other way.

At one time in my life, I was envious of people who were wealthy or important, but no more. I have learned that the person at the top may not always be having it so good. Again I quote the Apostle Paul in

1 Corinthians 4:9: *For I think that God hath set forth us the apostles last, as it were appointed to death: for we are made a spectacle unto the world, and to angels, and to men.*

If you are seeking greatness in God, you may not achieve greatness with humans. You may have to endure many unpleasant things.

The Office of Prophet

As we have already seen, the office of apostle is the highest ministry of the Church. The second ministerial office is that of the prophet. The office of prophet cannot be filled through a democratic election. A prophet is called of God and set apart by God. The person God picks to fill this office is not chosen on the basis of personality, education, or public standing. When God appoints a prophet in the land, the people there have nothing to do with it.

Old Testament Prophets

In the Old Testament, the position of a prophet was one of divine guide. He was sent by God to lead the people of Israel. The prophet at that time was also called a seer:

Beforetime in Israel, when a man went to enquire of God, thus he spake, Come, and let us go to the seer: for he that is now called a Prophet was beforetime called a Seer.

1 Samuel 9:9

The Hebrew word ra'ah — to see or to perceive — tells us what the ministry of the prophet is all about. Also, the word *chozeh* — beholder of visions — is used as that of a seer or a prophet.

The Bible lists 78 prophets and prophetesses. That would be sufficient for us to exhaust any area of knowledge relative to the prophets, if we were to study them in an in-depth way from Genesis to Revelation.

Adam

It is usually agreed that Adam was the first prophet.

And out of the ground the Lord God formed every beast of the field, and every fowl of the air; and brought them unto Adam to see what he would call them: and whatsoever Adam called every living creature, that was the name thereof.

Genesis 2:19

Adam moved in a spiritual sphere at that moment. He had some foreknowledge of what each animal would be like, so he named them according to the relationship they had with the rest of creation. This was a prophetic definition.

Enoch

A very remarkable prophet of the Old Testament is Enoch. Genesis 5:21 says: *And Enoch lived sixty and five years, and begat Methuselah.* The word *Methuselah* means "at his death the sending forth of waters."* Enoch was caught up with God when he was 365 years old, but his son Methuselah lived 969 years. Comparing the day Methuselah was born with the date of the Great Flood, you will discover that he died the year of the Flood. I believe he died the hour that the Flood began since his name means "at his death the sending forth of waters."

---

*Marked Reference Bible, Edited by J. Gilchrist Lawson, Zondervan Publishing House, Grand Rapids, Michigan.

More of Enoch's prophecy is found in the book of Jude, verses 14,15:

And Enoch also, the seventh from Adam, prophesied of these, saying, Behold, the Lord cometh with ten thousands of his saints,

To execute judgment upon all, and to convince all that are ungodly among them of all their ungodly deeds which they have ungodly committed, and of all their hard speeches which ungodly sinners have spoken against him.

This has not yet come to pass, so Enoch not only prophesied relative to his own son and the judgment that would come at his death 969 years later, but he said that God (in Jesus Christ) would one day come *with ten thousands of his saints.* Enoch was only the seventh man from Adam, yet imagine his knowing that Jesus was going to come back with many thousands of His saints. What a tremendous source of strength for seeing the future and predicting that which his mind had no capacity to know! This had to be a prophetic vision.

So prophets are not new and they are dramatic in their foretelling of what will come to pass. They have no earthly means of knowing what they foretell. Enoch made no calculations by the moon or stars or with the soothsayers. Only God told him. And he was such a godly man that he did not even see death, but was translated to heaven miraculously when he was 365 years old.

Noah

Another prophet of this magnitude is Noah. Genesis 6:8,9 says: *Noah found grace in the eyes of the Lord. These are the generations of Noah: Noah* was a just man and perfect in his generations, and Noah walked with God.

For over a hundred years Noah said there would be a flood of water that would cover the earth. He was a walking prophet, but he had to wait over a hundred years before his prophecy came to pass.

If you were a prophet or prophetess, a hundred years would be a long time to hang around with your prophecy not coming true. There would be plenty of people laughing at you and mocking you, saying it was all nonsense. It would be very discouraging.

But Noah walked with God. He believed what God had said for over a hundred years. (Some say it might have been as long as 120 years.) Then one day the clouds began to frown, the lightning began to flash, the thunder rolled, and the Flood came upon the face of the earth. This prophet of God said it would happen, and it did come to pass. That is what is meant by biblical prophet.

Anything that a true prophet foretells will come to pass because the Holy Spirit, Who told it to him, cannot lie. The Bible says that God cannot lie. *God is not a man, that he should lie; neither the son of man, that he should repent: hath he said, and shall he not do it? or hath he spoken, and shall he not make it good?* (Num. 23:19). So when one of God's prophets — a person who is anointed of God — speaks, it *will* come to pass.

Abraham

Abraham was another great prophet of God. In Genesis 24:6,7 we read about the time Abraham sent his servant to his home country to find a wife for his son Isaac:

217

Abraham said unto him (the servant), *Beware thou that thou bring not my son thither again.*

The Lord God of heaven, which took me from my father's house, and from the land of my kindred, and which spake unto me, and that sware unto me, saying, Unto thy seed will I give this land; he shall send his angel before thee, and thou shalt take a wife unto my son from thence.

Abraham said of God: "He shall do it." Now that is prophesying. He spoke to his servant and said, "Go back to my father's people — because God wants to keep this bloodstream pure — and there you will find a young woman who will be the bride for my son. She will be there and you will bring her back."

That is prophesying. Then when the beautiful young girl was brought back, Isaac was out in the field looking for her, which shows that he had faith in the prophecy made by his father. Isaac knew that what Abraham had prophesied would most certainly come to pass.

Jacob

Then there is Jacob. Genesis 49:1 says: *Jacob called unto his sons, and said, Gather yourselves together, that I may tell you that which shall befall you in the last days.* He continued then to tell them what kind of tribes they would head and what kind of lives they would lead. They are living almost that same disposition this very day.

Jacob told his sons that they would leave the land they were in and possess the land that belonged to them. He also told them just what kind of people they would be one to the other. Jacob was most definitely a prophet.

Joseph

Of Joseph, Genesis 41:15,16 says:

And Pharaoh said unto Joseph, I have dreamed a dream, and there is none that can interpret it: and I have heard say of thee, that thou canst understand a dream to interpret it.

And Joseph answered Pharaoh, saying, It is not in me: God shall give Pharaoh an answer of peace.

This dream was God's way of telling Pharaoh what He was about to do — that there would be seven years of plenty, followed by seven years of famine; and that if they did not prepare, all of them would die. And it came to pass just as Joseph had said it would.

Moses

Moses, we discover, wrote 475 verses of prophecy, which was quite a bit of prophesying. In Exodus 11:4,5 Moses said:

Thus saith the Lord, About midnight will I go out into the midst of Egypt:

And all the firstborn in the land of Egypt shall die, from the firstborn of Pharaoh that sitteth upon his throne, even unto the firstborn of the maidservant that is behind the mill; and all the firstborn of beasts.

It took courage for Moses to make a statement like that. Not only did he foretell what would happen, he even gave the exact hour it would take place. If there had been no dead firstborn children the next morning, Moses would have been a false prophet.

And there shall be a great cry throughout all the land of Egypt, such as there was none like it, nor shall be like it any more.

But against any of the children of Israel shall not a dog move his tongue, against man or beast: that ye may know how that the Lord doth put a difference between the Egyptians and Israel.

And all these thy servants shall come down unto me, and bow down themselves unto me, saying, Get thee out, and all the people that follow thee: and after that I will go out. And he went out from Pharaoh in a great anger.

Exodus 11:6-8

Moses was not a superman; he was just like you and me. He was a man, yielded to God and willing for those words to flow out of his mouth.

In Exodus 12:29-51 all this was completely, gloriously, mightily, and wonderfully fulfilled; so we would have to say that one of the greatest prophets of all times was this man called Moses.

Elijah

Elijah was well known in his day as a prophet of God. He was a seer; he saw the future and foretold what would come to pass before it happened.

In 1 Kings 17:1, Elijah had said to Ahab: *As the Lord God of Israel liveth, before whom I stand, there shall not be dew nor rain these years, but according to my word.* In other words, Elijah was saying: "It shall not rain unless I tell it to."

How would you like to make a statement today saying it would not rain again until you told it to?

In 1 Kings 18:41 we read: *Elijah said unto Ahab, Get thee up, eat and drink; for there is a sound of abundance of rain.* There had been no rain for over three years, but Elijah heard the sound of rain. There was no rain in the sky. Where was that sound? It was in Elijah's spirit. Verse 45 says: *And it came to pass in the meanwhile, that the heaven was black with clouds and wind, and there was a great rain.*

Isaiah

In his writings Isaiah reveals one of the greatest prophecies ever to come through the heart and lips of a human being: *Therefore the Lord himself shall give you a sign; Behold, a virgin shall conceive, and bear a son, and shall call his name Immanuel* (Is. 7:14).

Further in his writings, Isaiah tells how this One would come and die:

He is despised and rejected of men; a man of sorrows, and acquainted with grief: and we hid as it were our faces from him; he was despised, and we esteemed him not.

Surely he hath borne our griefs, and carried our sorrows: yet we did esteem him stricken, smitten of God, and afflicted. But he was wounded for our transgressions, he was bruised for our iniquities: the chastisement of our peace was upon him; and with his stripes we are healed.

All we like sheep have gone astray; we have turned every one to his own way; and the Lord hath laid on him the iniquity of us all. He was oppressed, and he was afflicted, yet he opened not his mouth: he is brought as a lamb to the slaughter, and as a sheep before her shearers is dumb, so he openeth not his mouth.

221

He was taken from prison and from judgment: and who shall declare his generation? for he was cut off out of the land of the living: for the transgression of my people was he stricken. And he made his grave with the wicked, and with the rich in his death; because he had done no violence, neither was any deceit in his mouth.

Yet it pleased the Lord to bruise him; he hath put him to grief: when thou shalt make his soul an offering for sin, he shall see his seed, he shall prolong his days, and the pleasure of the Lord shall prosper in his hand. He shall see of the travail of his soul, and shall be satisfied: by his knowledge shall my righteous servant justify many; for he shall bear their iniquities.

Therefore will I divide him a portion with the great, and he shall divide the spoil with the strong; because he hath poured out his soul unto death: and he was numbered with the transgressors; and he bare the sin of many, and made intercession for the transgressors.

Isaiah 53:3-12

The prophet Isaiah was telling of the ministry and sacrifice of Jesus 700 years before He was born, and every word was perfectly fulfilled.

David

Although we tend to think of David as a shepherd boy, or a warrior, or a poet, or a king, he is called a prophet in the New Testament. (Acts 1:16.) David wrote 385 verses of prophecy — 385 verses related to the future.

In Psalm 22:18 we read: *They part my garments among them, and cast lots upon my vesture.* Imagine

David's seeing Calvary and knowing what was going to take place there — how at Calvary they would divide Christ's raiment and gamble over it with lots. Imagine his seeing this scene in his spirit and knowing what was going to come to pass so far in the future.

Jeremiah

The last of the individual prophets we will consider is the great prophet, Jeremiah. In his book he spoke 985 verses of prophecy, beautifully foretelling future events — some of which were not good news. He foretold the Babylonian captivity of Judah, the things that would happen to them while in Babylon, and how a remnant would return one day. He told their whole story before it came to pass. His people were so angry with him that they threw him into a well to die. (Before you start praying to receive the ministry of a prophet, perhaps you should consider what the cost might be. You may not be cast into a well like Jeremiah was, but there are many other ways to be persecuted.)

One of the prophecies Jeremiah wrote is found in chapter 8, verse 11: *For they have healed the hurt of the daughter of my people slightly, saying, Peace, peace; when there is no peace.* This prophecy is fulfilled in 1 Thessalonians 5:3 relative to the Second Coming of our Lord and Savior Jesus Christ.

Most of Jeremiah's prophecies were related to the people of Israel because of their forsaking God, turning away from Him, backsliding, and going into bondage. It came to pass just as he had spoken.

From Jeremiah to Malachi, there are fifteen prophets who recorded their prophecies, and the things they wrote came to pass. That is significant indeed.

Prophets In Groups

In this study relative to the prophets, we have considered them in the singular. Now we will deal with them, not as individuals, but in groups, beginning with the seventy elders of Israel.

The Seventy

And the Lord came down in a cloud, and spake unto him (Moses), and took of the spirit that was upon him, and gave it unto the seventy elders (the men around Moses who supported him): and it came to pass, that, when the spirit rested upon them, they prophesied, and did not cease.

Numbers 11:25

God took the great prophet Moses and through him — possibly through the laying on of hands — commissioned seventy others to become prophets.

A Company of Prophets

After that thou shalt come to the hill of God, where is the garrison of the Philistines: and it shall come to pass, when thou art come thither to the city, that thou shalt meet a company of prophets coming down from the high place with a psaltery, and a tabret, and a pipe, and a harp, before them; and they (a whole company) shall prophesy.

And the Spirit of the Lord will come upon thee, and thou shalt prophesy with them, and shalt be turned into another man.

And let it be, when these signs are come unto thee . . . for God is with thee.

224

And thou shalt go down before me to Gilgal; and, behold, I will come down unto thee, to offer burnt offerings, and to sacrifice sacrifices of peace offerings: seven days shalt thou tarry, till I come to thee, and shew thee what thou shalt do.

And it was so, that when he (Saul) had turned his back to go from Samuel, God gave him another heart: and all those signs came to pass that day. And when they came thither to the hill, behold, a company of prophets met him; and the Spirit of God came upon him, and he prophesied among them.

1 Samuel 10:5-10

Here we find a company of men who prophesied the future as a group. They spoke to this young man who was to be the king of the land and told what would happen before it came to pass — and it happened just that way.

Sons of the Prophets

And Elijah said unto Elisha, Tarry here, I pray thee; for the Lord hath sent me to Bethel. And Elisha said unto him, As the Lord liveth, and as thy soul liveth, I will not leave thee. So they went down to Bethel. And the sons of the prophets that were at Bethel came forth to Elisha . . . .

2 Kings 2:2,3

This was a group called the "sons of the prophets." I suppose they had left their work (whatever it might have been) and had come to Bethel to a school that tutored in prophesying.

New Testament Writing Prophets

There were four New Testament writing prophets: Peter, Paul, James, and John.

Peter

On the day of Pentecost Peter preached to the people that they were seeing the fulfillment of *that which was spoken by the prophet Joel* (Acts 2:16). He also wrote many things relative to the signs and times of the coming of the Lord Jesus:

. . . *To an inheritance incorruptible, and undefiled, and that fadeth not away, reserved in heaven for you,*

Who are kept by the power of God through faith unto salvation ready to be revealed in the last time.

Wherein ye greatly rejoice, though now for a season, if need be, ye are in heaviness through manifold temptations:

That the trial of your faith, being much more precious than of gold that perisheth, though it be tried with fire, might be found unto praise and honour and glory at the appearing of Jesus Christ.

1 Peter 1:4-7

Paul

In his sermon to the Athenians on Mars Hill, Paul said:

Because he (God) hath appointed a day, in the which he will judge the world in righteousness by that man (Jesus) whom he hath ordained; whereof he hath given assurance unto all men, in that he hath raised him from the dead.

Acts 17:31

This was a prophecy. Paul wrote many other prophetic statements, such as 2 Corinthians 5:10: *For we must all appear before the judgment seat of Christ.* Here he prophesied that the Lord Jesus Christ would be the One to judge the world.

James

James was another of the writing prophets of the New Testament. In his epistle he wrote:

Go to now, ye rich men, weep and howl for your miseries that shall come upon you. Your riches are corrupted, and your garments are motheaten. Your gold and silver is cankered; and the rust of them shall be a witness against you, and shall eat your flesh as it were fire. Ye have heaped treasure together for the last days.

Behold, the hire of the labourers who have reaped down your fields, which is of you kept back by fraud, crieth: and the cries of them which have reaped are entered into the ears of the Lord of sabaoth (the Lord of battles).

Ye have lived in pleasure on the earth, and been wanton; ye have nourished your hearts, as in a day of slaughter. Ye have condemned and killed the just; and he doth not resist you. Be patient therefore, brethren, unto the coming of the Lord. Behold, the husbandman waiteth for the precious fruit of the earth.

James 5:1-7

We could write a whole chapter describing the prophecies of James, a remarkable person through whom the Holy Ghost was flowing.

John

The last of these four writing prophets of the New Testament was John, the Beloved. He writes:

The world passeth away, and the lust thereof: but he that doeth the will of God abideth forever.

Little children, it is the last time: and as ye have heard that antichrist shall come, even now are there

many antichrists; whereby we know it is the last
time.

1 John 2:17,18

Then in the Revelation we read:

*The Revelation of Jesus Christ, which God gave
unto him, to shew unto his servants things which
must shortly come to pass; and he sent and signified
it by his angel unto his servant John.*

Revelation 1:1

So these are the prophets who wrote in the New
Testament — Peter, Paul, James, and John — whose
ministries are recorded and remain with us until
today.

New Testament Speaking Prophets

There were other New Testament prophets who
did not write, but who spoke prophetically.

First, there was John the Baptist. We have
recorded instances where this man prophesied and
foretold events that were to come to pass. In
Matthew 3:11 as John was baptizing, he spoke
concerning the Messiah Who was to come:

*I indeed baptize you with water unto repen-
tance: but he that cometh after me is mightier than I,
whose shoes I am not worthy to bear: he shall baptize
you with the Holy Ghost, and with fire.*

In John 1:29,32-34 we find this record:

*The next day John seeth Jesus coming unto him,
and saith, Behold the Lamb of God, which taketh
away the sin of the world.*

*And John bare record, saying, I saw the Spirit
descending from heaven like a dove, and it abode
upon him. And I knew him not; but he that sent me to
baptize with water, the same said unto me, Upon*

whom thou shalt see the Spirit descending, and remaining on him, the same is he which baptizeth with the Holy Ghost. And I saw, and bare record that this is the Son of God.

Another New Testament prophet was Zacharias. In Luke 1:67-71 we read:

Zacharias was filled with the Holy Ghost, and prophesied, saying,

Blessed be the Lord God of Israel; for he hath visited and redeemed his people, and hath raised up an horn of salvation for us in the house of his servant David;

As he spake by the mouth of his holy prophets, which have been since the world began: that we should be saved from our enemies, and from the hand of all that hate us.

Simeon was another of these great old prophets. His prophecy at the temple to Joseph and Mary concerning the infant Jesus is recorded in Luke 2:25-35. God spoke through Simeon, telling what would certainly come to pass in the life of His Son.

These prophets mainly dealt with the life of Christ; but concerning the Church in the New Testament, we find others such as Agabus. The Bible says very little about this man, except that he was a prophet:

And in these days came prophets from Jerusalem unto Antioch.

And there stood up one of them named Agabus, and signified by the Spirit that there should be great dearth throughout all the world: which came to pass in the days of Claudius Caesar.

Acts 11:27,28

229

Then in Acts 21:10,11 we read:

And as we tarried there many days, there came down from Judaea a certain prophet, named Agabus.

And when he was come unto us, he took Paul's girdle, and bound his own hands and feet, and said, Thus saith the Holy Ghost, So shall the Jews at Jerusalem bind the man that owneth this girdle, and shall deliver him into the hands of the Gentiles.

Agabus made these two tremendous prophecies (he might have made hundreds, but these are the only two of which we have record), and both of them came to pass exactly as he predicted.

Also in the Acts of the Apostles we find an incident in which God spoke to Ananias and commanded him to go and minister to Saul of Tarsus:

The Lord said unto him (Ananias), Go thy way: for he (Saul) is a chosen vessel unto me, to bear my name before the Gentiles, and kings, and the children of Israel:

For I will shew him how great things he must suffer for my name's sake.

Acts 9:15,16

Receiving this prophecy from God that Saul was not a killer, but rather a servant of God, Ananias obeyed God and did as he was commanded. God told him exactly where to find Saul and what to say:

And the Lord said unto him, Arise, and go into the street which is called Straight, and enquire in the house of Judas for one called Saul, of Tarsus: for, behold, he prayeth . . .

And Ananias went his way, and entered into the house; and putting his hands on him said, Brother Saul, the Lord, even Jesus . . . hath sent me, that thou mightest receive thy sight, and be filled with the Holy Ghost.

Acts 9:11,17

We also notice in Acts 13:1,2 how the spirit of prophecy flowed through several people at one time:

Now there were in the church that was at Antioch certain prophets and teachers; as Barnabas, and Simeon that was called Niger, and Lucius of Cyrene, and Manaen, which had been brought up with Herod the tetrarch, and Saul.

As they ministered to the Lord, and fasted, the Holy Ghost said, Separate me Barnabas and Saul for the work whereunto I have called them.

Here the Bible says that in this particular church there were certain prophets — and it names them — who foretold the future. I assume that nearly all churches have deacons or elders; but how many churches today claim to have apostles or prophets? They should. Apostles and prophets are as much a ministry of the Church as elders and deacons. I believe God is ready to bring them out and have His glorious power manifested on the face of this earth in a way that we have never known before.

Sometimes prophets speak only to individuals as in Acts, chapter 5, when Peter spoke to Ananias and Sapphira. At other times prophecy is directed to a group. For instance, in Revelation, chapter 2, one prophecy was directed to each one of the seven churches through the prophet John.

Sometimes prophecy is directed to an entire nation. Many times the whole nation of Israel received prophecies from God. It is possible for God to speak to our whole nation at one time and to say,

231

"America, thus saith God to you . . . ." A prophecy can be for one person, for a group, for a nation, or it can be for the whole world. God said to Jeremiah: *Before I formed thee in the belly I knew thee; and before thou camest forth out of the womb I sanctified thee, and I ordained thee a prophet unto the nations* (Jer. 1:5). Jeremiah was a prophet not just to Israel, but to the nations — and God ordained it so.

Prophetesses

There is very little that has not already been said about the subject of female involvement in the ministry. In many instances, I feel that God does not see male nor female; He sees into hearts and spirits, knowing the desires within a person.

Because my father was not converted until he was an elderly man, my mother was the spiritual force in our home. I learned to respect the spiritual power of a woman as I grew up.

When my grandfather suffered a stroke and was in a wheelchair, paralyzed, the preachers prayed for him, but nothing happened. Then my mother gathered a group of prayer ladies together around his chair and began to weep and travail before the Lord, and God healed him. My grandfather came out of that wheelchair completely healed and lived a good, strong, totally healthy life for the next forty years. The night he died at 87 years of age, he ate a good dinner and went to bed about nine o'clock. When we heard a little noise in the bedroom and went in to check on him, he had already gone to be with the Lord. Anyone who says that God does not use women has not studied history or the Bible.

God wants us to judge ministries, not people. If the Spirit of the Lord and divine words are flowing from a person — man or woman — who are we to say it is wrong?

There have been a number of prophetesses in the Scriptures. God has used women in many ways, both conventional and unconventional.

Miriam

And Miriam the prophetess, the sister of Aaron, took a timbrel in her hand; and all the women went out after her with timbrels and with dances.

Exodus 15:20

Here the Bible recognizes Miriam as a prophetess. A prophetess is only one thing — one who prophesies. Of that, there can be no doubt.

Deborah

Deborah, a prophetess, the wife of Lapidoth, she judged Israel at that time.

Judges 4:4

Deborah was both a prophetess and a judge in the land of Israel. It might have been that God could find no one else to do it.

Huldah

So Hilkiah the priest, and Ahikam, and Achbor, and Shaphan, and Asahiah, went unto Huldah the prophetess, . . . (now she dwelt in Jerusalem in the college;) and they communed with her.

2 Kings 22:14

Huldah is also mentioned in 2 Chronicles 34:22:

. . . they that the King had appointed, went to Huldah the prophetess . . . and they spake to her to

233

that effect. And she answered them, *Thus saith the Lord God of Israel* . . . .

All these men — the priests of God — went to Huldah, the prophetess, in order to hear from God.

False Prophetess

In Nehemiah 6:14 we read these words:

My God, think thou upon Tobiah and Sanballat according to these their works, and on the prophetess Noadiah, and the rest of the prophets, that would have put me in fear.

Here we have a false prophetess, a prophetess of the Devil, a woman who had given herself over to the Devil.

Isaiah's Wife

Another very interesting fact is recorded by Isaiah. It seems that his wife was a prophetess. He writes: *And I went unto the prophetess; and she conceived, and bare a son. Then said the Lord to me, Call his name Maher-shalal-hash-baz* (Is. 8:3). (I'd have called him Junior!)

Anna

In the New Testament we have a prophetess of the Lord named Anna:

And there was one Anna, a prophetess, the daughter of Phanuel, of the tribe of Aser: she was of a great age, and had lived with an husband seven years from her virginity;

And she was a widow of about fourscore and four years, which departed not from the temple, but served God with fastings and prayers night and day.

And she coming in that instant gave thanks likewise unto the Lord, and spake of him (the baby

Jesus) *to all them that looked for redemption in Jerusalem.*

Luke 2:36-38

Prophets Today

We find in the Word that God has used men and women to be His prophets and prophetesses, and the God Who produced this ministry throughout the Bible wants to do the same today in an even greater way. He wishes in these last days to breathe upon the total Church of the Lord Jesus and speak to us through these submitted and dedicated vessels, that we might know things which surely shall come to pass and that we might have direction.

The carnal mind does not know what it ought to do, but the spirit does. We are saying in our hearts: "Oh, God, send us prophets and prophetesses that we might better know what we should do for You in the days in which we live." I am sure our hearts are open for God to reveal unto us His chosen prophets and prophetesses.

And there *are* prophets today!

I lived for many years with Howard Carter, who fulfilled the office of prophet. At times it seemed somewhat frightening to live with such a man. He knew so many things about so many people. Never would he leave these prophecies to doubt. He would write them down and circulate them to make sure people knew what he was talking about. The accuracy with which he prophesied was astounding.

As I have already related in this book, Rev. Carter knew in advance how he would meet me and the exact words I would say when we met as strangers. He circulated that prophecy in England until there were probably twenty-five preachers carrying a prophetic record of how Howard Carter would meet a stranger from afar and the very words that stranger would speak when they met. Rev. Carter was not the least bit surprised when I walked up to him and spoke those words. On the other hand, I was shocked at my behavior. Here was a man I had never met and knew nothing about, yet I had just told him that God had sent me to work with him. And work together we did for many years, until Rev. Carter went home to heaven.

God does have prophets today. He is speaking to people, but much of the Body of Christ is ignorant of this fact and not desirous of it. There are only a few things that can keep us from knowing the future. One is sin; another is unbelief.

Unbelief cuts off the miracle power of God. In churches where the people say God cannot act, He only shakes His head and says, "You're right. I can't act here." What we must do is say, "Lord, if You wish to give me one of these ministries in the Body of Christ, I accept it." By doing this, you will see more of the power of God than ever before in your life.

Perhaps there is nothing so exciting as prophecy. In these last days we must have the prophet's ministry at work among us. All kinds of people will be reading the stars and predicting future events. The Devil will be out to fool as many people as he can regarding the future, so God's people must take their place against him.

Don't be afraid of the future. No matter what happens, I guarantee you a greater move of the supernatural than you have ever seen before. Let's get ready for it. Let's seek it. Let's love it. I know that the God of heaven is going to bless us in it, and I am ready for His blessing! Let the ministry of the prophet be heard in the land!

The Office of Evangelist

The evangelist is a proclaimer of the Gospel. That is his purpose of ministry, and he does not deviate from it. He simply preaches the love and forgiveness of God and the salvation that is available to all through His Son Jesus Christ. When he preaches this simple Gospel message, people receive salvation.

An evangelist is a gift from God to the Church. A person cannot go to Bible school and study to become an evangelist.

If you need an evangelist, call upon the Holy Ghost and He will send you one — Jesus said He would:

The harvest truly is plenteous, but the labourers are few;

Pray ye therefore the Lord of the harvest, that he will send forth labourers into his harvest.

Matthew 9:37,38

Philip

The church in Jerusalem had picked this man Philip, as one of the seven deacons who would serve the apostles and the other disciples. He was described as being *of honest report, full of the Holy Ghost and wisdom* (Acts 6:3). But God had some other plans for Philip. Though Philip had no training as an evangelist, that is the office God called him to fill, and a whole city came to God because of his evangelism:

237

Then Philip went down to the city of Samaria, and preached Christ unto them.

And the people with one accord gave heed unto those things which Philip spake, hearing and seeing the miracles which he did.

For unclean spirits, crying with loud voice, came out of many that were possessed with them: and many taken with palsies, and that were lame, were healed.

And there was great joy in that city.

Acts 8:5-8

Later we see that Philip left Jerusalem and moved to the oceanside at Caesarea where he became known as God's evangelist:

The next day we that were of Paul's company departed, and came unto Caesarea: and we entered into the house of Philip the evangelist, which was one of the seven; and abode with him.

Acts 21:8

Timothy

In 2 Timothy 4:5 Paul wrote to the young preacher Timothy: *Watch thou in all things, endure afflictions, do the work of an evangelist, make full proof of thy ministry.* This means Paul was very conscious of the fact that God had laid His hands upon that young man, Timothy, and had called him to save souls. So he admonished him to do the work of an evangelist. Paul was saying to him: "Now God has given you this ministry gift, and I want you to make full proof of it. Get out there and get those people saved!"

The Need For Evangelists

The number of evangelists today is not large. I believe we should pray for God to give us more. As an evangelist, nobody has to give you a place to preach. When God calls you to do something, just go out and start doing it.

The morning I left home to preach, I had no idea where I was going; we headed north toward the country. In the afternoon we stopped at a little country schoolhouse and started a revival meeting there. We stayed several weeks and baptized 67 adults. A church was established. Two missionaries later went out to Africa from the crusade. Also one pastor entered the ministry.

Evangelists get discouraged sometimes when they go to a church and fail to get many people saved. The reason is they are doing their evangelizing in the wrong place. You cannot expect to grow corn if you plant the seed around the church altar. Evangelists need to go out and plant their seed where the sinners are, then they will reap a harvest. We need to pray that God will give us some great evangelists, and that could mean you.

The Office of Pastor

A pastor is a shepherd. The Greek word *poimen* occurs 17 times in the New Testament. Only one time is it translated "pastor," which is in Ephesians 4:11. The other 16 times, it is translated "shepherd." So in Ephesians 4:11 Paul is saying that the pastor is to be the shepherd of his flock, of his church.

Matthew 9:36 says: *When he (Jesus) saw the multitudes, he was moved with compassion on them, because they fainted, and were scattered abroad, as*

239

sheep having no shepherd. Jesus is the chief Shepherd, the chief Pastor. He saw the multitudes and was moved with compassion.

This demonstrates the pastor's heart. There are some people who cannot see a multitude. All they see is a crowd, and they don't like crowds; they don't like being jostled and pushed. But Jesus did not see only a crowd of people; He saw a multitude in need, and He was moved by their needs. He saw that they fainted and were scattered, like sheep with no shepherd. They needed a pastor.

The Hebrew word *ra'ah* means "to tend sheep." In the Old Testament this word is translated "pastor" eight times, as in Jeremiah 2:8:

The priests said not, Where is the Lord? and they that handle the law knew me not: the pastors (those who were supposed to be tending God's sheep) *also transgressed against me, and the prophets prophesied by Baal* (a heathen god), *and walked after things that do not profit.*

In Jeremiah 3:15 God said:

And I will give you pastors according to mine (own) *heart, which shall feed you with knowledge and understanding.*

This is the ministry of a pastor: to feed the flock with knowledge and understanding, to feed the souls of all who come by the Spirit of God. And it need not be just a few. It can be 6, or 600, or 6,000. In fact, the more people there are, the more inspiration a pastor can get and the better he can feed them. It arouses that force and anointing within him and enables him to feed them well.

240

I have heard people comment that a particular church congregation is too large for the pastor to handle effectively. However, he can pastor only one person at a time. When he stands and speaks, he is speaking to one person. When he feeds a group of any size, he is feeding them only one at a time.

Think how it must have been in the first church in Jerusalem. There were 3,000 saved in one day and 5,000 saved another day. Acts 2:47 says: . . . *the Lord added to the church daily such as should be saved.* There must have been 50,000 members in that church!

A young man named Charles Spurgeon went to London when he was only 17 years of age, and in a few months was pastoring a very large congregation. Within a year or two, it was the largest congregation in England. Spurgeon held that congregation in the Metropolitan Tabernacle in London until he died. He was a good shepherd; he had a pastor's heart. He wanted to feed people, to heal the wounded.

In addition to a shepherd, the Bible also speaks of hirelings — people who say they are pastors. In John's Gospel, Jesus said:

I am the good shepherd: the good shepherd giveth his life for the sheep.

But he that is an hireling, and not the shepherd, whose own the sheep are not, seeth the wolf coming, and leaveth the sheep, and fleeth: and the wolf catcheth them, and scattereth the sheep.

The hireling fleeth, because he is an hireling, and careth not for the sheep.

John 10:11-13

241

There is a great difference between someone who has been hired and someone whom God has commissioned. A real pastor is commissioned by God to do his job, and he will pastor even if he never gets a dime. He will keep doing it, if he never gets any appreciation. Why? Because God told him to do it. A hireling, on the other hand, will quit if he does not get exactly what he wants.

The distinguishing mark is the pastor's heart. A shepherd's heart cannot be fabricated. It cannot be received at Bible school. A shepherd's heart comes only from God. Either you have it, or you do not.

The Office of Teacher

A teacher of the Word can be located in one place, or he can travel. The office of teacher carries a very special anointing for opening people's understanding of God's Word.

Howard Carter filled this ministerial office. There was nothing in the Bible that he could not simplify so that even a child could understand. For a number of years he and I lived and traveled together with great unity and blessing, and I was always amazed at his ability to teach. In our meetings, he would teach first; then I would operate as the evangelist. After he had finished teaching the saints, I would bring the Gospel message of salvation to those who were not yet Christians.

Rev. Carter was recognized as one of the great Bible teachers in the world; but if we had a houseful of sinners, he could not get even one of them saved. He was not called to be an evangelist. That is why God fit us together; we could work well together to edify His Church. We made a great team! I had an ability for evangelism, not an ability I had learned, but one that God had put in my heart — the ability to have compassion on the lost, to bring them in, and to give them to Him; Howard Carter, on the other hand, had been given the gift of teaching.

You might be surprised at the number of great Bible teachers who are almost illiterate. If you ask them a question about philosophy or some other subject, they are at a loss; but they can open a Bible and simply amaze you with their knowledge and understanding. As they give an exposition on the Word of God, it is truth pouring forth from them. Though they have little or no education, they are anointed to teach the Word of God. On the other hand, you may meet a learned professor who cannot understand a single page in the whole Bible.

All the education in the world will not make a teacher of God's Word. A teacher is a person who has been set in the Body of Christ by God for one specific purpose: to teach the Word.

17
Elders, Deacons, Helps, and Governments

Having studied the fivefold ministry gifts — apostles, prophets, evangelists, pastors, and teachers — we now come to the portion of laborers in the Body of Christ who are set aside by these spiritual leaders.

The Office of Elder

The first we will deal with is the elder, or bishop. First Timothy 3:1 states: *This is a true saying, If a man desire the office of a bishop* (or elder), *he desireth a good work.* It is good to desire the office of elder — not the title, but the ministry it involves.

First Timothy 5:17-19 reveals how the elder is to function in the Body of Christ:

Let the elders that rule well be counted worthy of double honour, especially they who labour in the word and doctrine.

For the scripture saith, Thou shalt not muzzle the ox that treadeth out the corn. And, The labourer is worthy of his reward.

Against an elder receive not an accusation, but before two or three witnesses.

In Acts 20:17 we read: *And from Miletus he* (Paul) *sent to Ephesus, and called the elders of the church.* Paul called them together for a consultation about their ministry — what they should do and how they should work in the Church.

In James 5:14,15 we read:

Is any sick among you? let him call for the elders of the church; and let them pray over him, anointing him with oil in the name of the Lord:

And the prayer of faith shall save the sick, and the Lord shall raise him up.

Acts 14:23 states: And when they had ordained them elders in every church, and had prayed with fasting, they commended them to the Lord, on whom they believed.

These elders were men of the Church who were mature, both physically and spiritually. Such men were ordained or anointed and set aside for service by the laying on of hands.

In Titus 1:5,6 Paul wrote:

For this cause left I thee in Crete, that thou shouldest set in order the things that are wanting, and ordain elders in every city, as I had appointed thee:

If any be blameless, the husband of one wife, having faithful children not accused of riot or unruly.

Here Paul was showing us the responsibilities and qualifications of these elders. It is good to obey the Lord in everything, especially when it concerns elders, because they are the ones who function in the spiritual part of the Church.

In our church there are about fifty elders, who visit church members each week. When a member of our church is ill, the elders will go quickly and joyfully to minister to them. We receive good reports of how God heals and blesses through the work of our elders.

Verses 7-9 continue:

For a bishop (or elder) must be blameless, as the steward of God; not selfwilled, not soon angry, not given to wine, no striker, not given to filthy lucre (that is, not a lover of money);

But a lover of hospitality (one who invites people into his home and ministers to them), a lover of good men (associates with good people), sober, just, holy, temperate; holding fast the faithful word as he hath been taught.

Notice this last phrase: . . . *as he hath been taught.* The apostle, prophet, evangelist, pastor, or teacher whom God has set in the Church takes those in the Church and teaches them. As verse 9 continues, an elder is taught *that he may be able by sound doctrine* (as he has been taught) *both to exhort and to convince the gainsayers* (those who come against the Body). This is the role of the elder: a spiritual overseer in the Church, involved in blessing the people spiritually.

The Office of Deacon

Next we have the office of deacon. The first deacons were chosen in Acts, chapter 6:

And in those days, when the number of the disciples was multiplied, there arose a murmuring of the Grecians against the Hebrews, because their widows were neglected in the daily ministration . . .

Wherefore, brethren, look ye out among you seven men of honest report, full of the Holy Ghost and wisdom, whom we may appoint over this business.

But we will give ourselves continually to prayer, and to the ministry of the word (vv. 1,3,4).

You probably know the rest of the story. They chose seven men to be deacons: . . . *and when they* had prayed, they laid their hands on them (v. 6). As deacons, these men were given jobs to do in the Church.

In 1 Timothy 3:8-12 we read:

Likewise must the deacons be grave, not double-tongued, not given to much wine, not greedy of filthy lucre; holding the mystery of the faith in a pure conscience.

And let these also first be proved (not novices); then let them use the office of a deacon, being found blameless.

Even so must their wives be grave, not slanderers, sober, faithful in all things.

Let the deacons be the husbands of one wife, ruling their children and their own houses well.

As qualifications for both the eldership and the deaconship, God said these men should be capable of ruling their own house. Americans have been taught very little about this subject, and it grieves me.

Once I was preaching in what was then the largest full Gospel church in the world — an enormous church in Stockholm, Sweden. While I was there, the pastor told me a very exciting story. Shortly before I arrived, he had resigned the church, though he was its founder. One day he stood before the congregation and said very simply, "I resign." When the board asked, "Why?" he answered, "One of my children (he had eleven) is not living for God. I will resign and stay at home in prayer until he is saved."

Immediately, that church body set themselves as one to pray for his son. What was that boy to do when 6,000 church members started praying? He got saved in a hurry!

Here was a man who ruled his house well, which is how a deacon is to be.

My wife and I witnessed a very interesting occurrence in Puerto Rico. As we were preaching there, a missionary came by the church to visit. He stood during the service and, rather than preaching, gave his life's testimony. He said, "I was called to be a missionary in India. While there my wife fell in love with another man and left me. Now I am alone as I go out preaching the Word. I've come down here because I love you and I'm going to preach the Word to you. How glad I am to be with you."

The pastor of that church stopped him and said, "Sit back down. A man who can't control one little woman is surely not going to preach to my people. You can just go back to America." (Those people are called "natives," but they know how to operate their church.)

The Bible says that a deacon must be faithful in all things, the husband of one wife, ruling his children and his house well. *For they that have used the office of a deacon well purchase to themselves a good degree, and great boldness in the faith which is in Christ Jesus* (1 Tim. 3:13). Deaconship is a good work. The Lord expects a deacon to be an example to the people in his church.

The Ministry of Helps

Now we come to the ministry of helps. There has been much confusion about this subject since very little has been taught about it.

249

The New Testament is filled with examples of helps in action. The word *helps* in Acts 27:17 speaks of the ropelike cable that sailors used to wrap around the ship during a storm: *. . . they used helps, undergirding the ship . . . .* The ministry of helps is what God wraps around us to hold us together in our stormy times.

The Bible mentions seven people who ministered in this area of helps. For example, there is Phebe. In Romans 16:1,2 Paul says: *I commend unto you Phebe our sister, which is a servant of the church . . . That ye receive her in the Lord . . . for she hath been a succourer* (helper) *of many, and of myself also.* Phebe was a helper. She carried the book of Romans to Rome for Paul at his request. Though she was not a preacher, Phebe helped spread the Word.

Lydia was another helper who supported Paul. We find in Acts 16:14,15 how she provided lodging in her home in Philippi for Paul and his group.

In the Old Testament there were two men who held up the arms of Moses during a battle. (Ex. 17:8-12.) As long as Moses held up his hands, there was victory for the children of Israel; but when he became weary and let them fall, they began to lose. So Aaron and Hur held up Moses' tired arms and helped win the victory. They were helpers; Moses could not function without them.

No man of God can function without helpers. I am surrounded with helpers; and when we get to heaven, they may get a bigger reward than I. That will be God's business, not mine.

You may ask, "Why would they get a larger reward?" Because they may have been more faithful in their helping than I have been in my ministering.

It was the Lord Jesus Who said that if you give even a drink of water to a prophet, you shall receive a prophet's reward for helping. (Matt. 10:41,42.) There are big stakes involved for being a helper.

The secretaries in my office are helpers. The person who runs our printing press is a helper. Without these helpers, I would be unable to minister.

All those who supported Paul's ministry, financially or otherwise, were helpers.

When King David went out to defeat the enemy, there went before him a standard-bearer who carried his shield. That person was a helper. He may not have been a strong man, but all he was required to do was to carry that shield. He was a helper, and that ministry is important.

Though God has appointed only a few apostles and prophets, he has thousands of helpers. These helpers are very important to God, and they have their reward in heaven. There are many bricks in a brick wall, and we cannot tell which is the most important. Each brick contributes to the strength of the whole wall. That is the function of a helper.

Through our television outreach, one lesson will be broadcast to perhaps several million people. It could not be done without the help of the cameramen and all the technicians. They are helpers.

The work of the Lord *must* have helpers. Any time we downgrade such helps, we are in danger of failure. Helps is a ministry that was placed in the Church by God. As you study the whole of the Bible, you will see that all these helps are necessary. You can even go a step further and say that the giving of the tithe is a help. All of us are helpers in one way or another. Though the widow gives only three or four dollars and the businessman gives a hundred dollars, both are helpers — one is just as important as the other.

There is one particular family in our church that is always asking for names of people they can visit in the hospital. They are helpers, and God loves helpers. God has placed helpers in the Church, and we must keep them there.

Governments

In 1 Corinthians 12:28 the Greek word for *governments* is *kubernesis,* meaning "to steer or to guide." This word *governments* means the steering committee; it has no reference to power or to ruling. Those who possess knowledge to steer a church and guide it around its problems become the governments of that church.

Within a church, there are many kinds of operations, all kinds of groups and committees. To build a new building, you choose a building committee. This is an example of church government.

You may ask, "Why does God want all of this?" Because He wants order. For everything to run smoothly, there must be organization. God wants church government to be well oiled with the Holy Ghost. This means that mature men and women can bless the church by being set aside to do certain things within the church, to operate the church in the way it ought to be operated.

Each Has A Place

These nine offices of ministry which God has set in the Church have a purpose. All are necessary for a well-ordered Church, and in these last days each of us has a place in the Church. We should ask ourselves every day, "What can I do to fit more perfectly into the divine pattern that God has planned for the Church of the Lord Jesus Christ?"

Each of us has a place in God's Church, a job to fulfill. The Lord is waiting for us to move into our nitch and do our best for Him.

18
Combinations of Ministries

When God gives ministerial gifts to the Body of Christ, He may give more than one gift to the same person. For example, some people may fill a dual ministry, such as pastor and teacher. They can pastor a church magnificently, then proceed to a Bible college and open the Word of God to the student body in a splendid fashion. Others serve as both pastor and evangelist. They pastor their churches on Sunday; then go out on Monday, hold revival meetings, and cause hundreds of people to receive the Lord Jesus Christ.

This combination of ministries occurs, not because a person seeks these gifts, but because God has bestowed them upon him. He obtains them without struggling, without trying; they just flow from him under the anointing of the Holy Spirit.

In the church at Antioch, there were both prophets and teachers. Again I cite Acts 13:1,2 as an example:

Now there were in the church that was at Antioch certain prophets and teachers; as Barnabas, and Simeon that was called Niger, and Lucius of Cyrene, and Manaen, which had been brought up with Herod the tetrarch, and Saul.

As they ministered to the Lord, and fasted, the Holy Ghost said, Separate me Barnabas and Saul for the work whereunto I have called them.

God was calling out Barnabas and Saul (or Paul) that they might go as a pair to proclaim the Gospel of the Lord Jesus Christ. Paul was an apostle, and very likely Barnabas was also; but they were endowed with teaching abilities, so that wherever they went, they taught the truth of God. You will notice in Paul's writings that he was a tremendous teacher. Read Ephesians or Romans or Galatians, and you will see that Paul was a master teacher. Yet he was an evangelist, taking the Gospel throughout the then-known world; and he was a pastor, establishing churches and seeing them developed. (He stayed in one church for two years.)

As an apostle, Paul was a combination of all these ministries — performing every ministry in the Church with excellence.

One combination of ministries that is particularly interesting involved deaconship. There are two examples of ministry I wish to share with you: Stephen and Philip.

In Acts 6:5 the Church chose Stephen, *a man full of faith and of the Holy Ghost,* to be one of the original seven deacons. Then verse 8 says: *And Stephen, full of faith and power, did great wonders and miracles among the people.* Though Stephen had been chosen and set apart as a deacon by the apostleship of the Church, God had something more for him. The church leaders looked at Stephen and saw a good waiter; God looked at him and saw much more. He saw a man who would lay hands on the sick, cast out devils, and do miracles.

In Acts 6:9,10 we read:

There arose certain of the synagogue, which is called the synagogue of the Libertines, and Cyrenians, and Alexandrians, and of them of Cilicia and of Asia, disputing with Stephen (not with the apostles, but with Stephen).

And they were not able to resist the wisdom and the spirit by which he spake.

We find that this man Stephen had much more going for him than just deaconship.

Philip also had been chosen as one of the original seven deacons, but God did something more with him: He made Philip into a tremendous evangelist. We read in Acts 8:5-8 how Philip moved a whole city at one time:

Philip went down to the city of Samaria, and preached Christ unto them.

And the people with one accord gave heed unto those things which Philip spake, hearing and seeing the miracles which he did. For unclean spirits, crying with loud voice, came out of many that were possessed with them: and many taken with palsies, and that were lame, were healed.

And there was great joy in that city.

Man said to Philip, "You wait on tables," but Philip did more than that. He performed the ministry of an evangelist. What a tremendous difference!

Men may select us for one thing, but the final selection is up to God — and when God selects us for a job, it is good. I believe, too, that God can enlarge the ministry within us. We begin at one level of ministry; and after we have proven ourselves at that, God adds to the anointing in our lives.

The opposite is true regarding a person who attempts to fill an office of ministry to which God has not called him. Again, I use Smith Wigglesworth as an illustration.

Wigglesworth was never called to pastor; he was called as an evangelist. When he had a church in England, he only stood in the back and handed out song books; his wife did all the preaching. Yet he could travel to South Africa or Switzerland or Scandinavia and minister to thousands of people with an anointing that just poured from him.

After his wife died, Wigglesworth gave up his pastorate; but he never surrendered his call to evangelism. When God places a ministry in an anointed vessel, it is normally there for life. Even while in his 80s, Wigglesworth could still preach for only three minutes and get people saved.

Pastoring and preaching are two entirely different aspects of ministry. Not every great pastor is a great preacher. In one of the largest churches where I have preached, the pastor was not a preacher. Anyone on the front row could have preached better than he. All he did was stand in the pulpit and minister love to his congregation. He was a true shepherd to his church flock. A pastor's love cannot be fabricated; and unless God gives you a shepherd's heart, you will never be able to fill that office.

You may ask, *How can I know the office of ministry that God has called me to fill?*

This is a common question and one that is very simple to answer. If a person has a ministry, his ministry will flow out of him and produce the proper fruit. Ministry is evidence, and it just makes a way and a place for itself.

A pear tree does not ask what it is; it just grows pears. There is no doubt about it: It is not a banana tree; its leaves are not the same and its fruit is not the same. People will know what you are by the fruit you produce. As you seek the Lord, pray in the Spirit, and study God's Word, the ministry gift that God has placed in you will surface without your having to force it out.

Start Where You Are

Let me close this study with some simple words of counsel. Many times we want to begin our ministry with something very big; but very seldom will it come about that way. A person does not conduct the Boston Symphony Orchestra the very first day he is handed a baton. A little preparatory work is required first.

I admonish you that as you are reaching out to minister for God, begin by doing everything your hand finds to do. If you feel in your heart that God is going to use you in a great way, do something close by. If you feel the call to be a pastor or teacher, start by teaching a Sunday school class. You will find out right away if you have the ability. If that little class falls to pieces, I suggest that you not try to pastor a church because you failed the elementary pastoring session.

Do you feel a call to evangelism? Then go out into your own neighborhood, to your neighbors and friends, and get somebody saved. Go across town to someone you have never seen before and see if you can lead them to Jesus. Go into the nursing homes and talk to the people there, or into the jail and preach to them.

The first place I preached was in a prison. I never knew whether I was worth anything to the Kingdom; I was just struggling to do my best. I preached in prison a few times, preached in a ladies' prayer meeting, then went up into the country to a little country schoolhouse and preached there.

From there I moved on to another little country schoolhouse, then another, and another. It looked as if I was going to get educated at a country schoolhouse. I seldom preached in a church. Nobody invited me. I just preached in front of a schoolhouse.

In one place the next day after I preached, the farmer where I was staying asked: "Did you enjoy your bed?"

I said, "Yes."

"Did you enjoy your food?"

"Yes."

"Then go feed my pigs."

I said, "But I'm the preacher."

"I know that; but around here if you don't work, you don't eat. If you want to come back to the table again, you'll have to go feed my hogs."

I was born in New Orleans and reared in Mobile, Alabama, and Panama City, Florida. I knew what ham was, but that was about all I knew about pigs!

The farmer showed me the slop bucket. (I almost got sick just at the name of it!) The bucket they used was just an old oilcan with a piece of wire across the top for a handle. The food for the pigs was so heavy that it slopped over the top and onto my clothes. (I guess that's why they were called slop buckets.) I had only two pairs of pants — one on and one off! It was very embarrassing to have to wash my clothes before I could change. Finally, I lay down in a cornfield and cried. I said, "Now I know I'm the prodigal son. I've got all the evidence of it. I'm in the pigpen, and I'd like to get out."

The Lord spoke up in my heart and said, "If you'll be faithful, I'll bless you."

Sometimes our beginnings are not easy. I preached for a whole week and the total offering I received amounted to 26 cents! There were no nickels, just 26 pennies.

You have to start where you are. Before you try to trust God for a seven-tier cake, trust Him for a doughnut. It gets easier as you get higher. But start where you are. Don't wait for the doors to open, or you will die of old age while you are waiting! Create doors all around you. There is so much that needs to be done, so get started!

Appendix
The Charisma Through The Centuries

Current history is better understood in the perspective of the related past. The gifts of the Spirit, including speaking in tongues, have appeared and reappeared in the Christian Church from its conception, having been a witness in every branch of Christendom.

In History

1. Dr. Philip Schaff, the well-known church historian, in his *History of the Christian Church*, Volume 1, writes:

   "The speaking with tongues, however, was not confined to the Day of Pentecost. Together with the other extraordinary spiritual gifts which distinguished this age above the succeeding periods of more quiet and natural development, this gift also, though to be sure in a modified form, perpetuated itself in the apostolic church. We find traces of it still in the second and third centuries."

2. Irenaeus (A.D. 115-202) was a pupil of Polycarp, who was a disciple of the Apostle John. In *Against Heresies*, Book V, he wrote:

   "In like manner do we also hear many brethren in the Church who possess prophetic gifts and who through the Spirit speak all kinds of languages, and bring mysteries of God, whom also the apostles term spiritual."

3. "The Latin church father, Tertullian (A.D. 160-220), writing against Marcion, said:

'Let Marcion then exhibit, as gifts of his god, some prophets, such as have not spoken by human sense, but with the Spirit of God, such as have predicted things to come, and have made manifest the secrets of the heart; let him produce a psalm, a vision, a prayer — only let it be by the spirit, in an ecstasy, that is, in a rapture, whenever an interpretation of tongues has occurred to him.' Now all these signs (or spiritual gifts) are forthcoming from my side without any difficulty, and they agree, too, with the rules, and the dispensations, and the instructions of the Creator." (Dr. *William Smith's Dictionary of the Bible*, vol. 4, p. 3310).

4. "St. Pachomius (A.D. 292-346), the Egyptian founder of the first Christian monastery, is said to have enjoyed the use of the Greek and Latin languages which he sometimes miraculously spoke, having never learned them. This gift was given to him at times after special prayer for the power to meet an immediate need" (*Lives of the Saints,* Alban Butler, 1756).

5. "The history of the Waldenses in the 12th and 13th centuries reveals not only a devotion of the Bible reading and a desire to follow the primitive purity of the New Testament Church, but also that both healing and speaking in unknown languages were experienced from time to time in their midst" (*Gift of Tongues,* Alexandria Mockie, p. 27).

6. John Calvin (1509-1564) wrote in his *Commentary on the Epistles of Paul the Apostle to the Corinthians*, Volume 1, p. 437:

". . . there are at present great theologians, who declaim against them with furious zeal. As it is certain that the Holy Spirit has here honored the use of tongues with never-dying praise, we may very readily gather, what is the kind of spirit that actuates those reformers, who level as many reproaches as they can against the pursuit of them."

This particular comment is in reference to Paul's statement in 1 Corinthians 14:5: *I would that ye all spake with tongues.*

7. In *Souer's History of the Christian Church*, Volume 3, p. 206, the following statement is found:

"Dr. Martin Luther was a prophet, evangelist, speaker in tongues and interpreter, in one person, endowed with all the gifts of the Holy Spirit."

8. Regarding Dwight L. Moody, here are a few quotations from *Trails and Triumphs of Faith*, 1875 Edition, p. 402, by the Reverend R. Boyd, D.D. Rev. Boyd of the Baptist faith was a very intimate friend of the famous evangelist. He wrote:

"When I got to the rooms of the Young Men's Christian Association (Victoria Hall, London), I found the meeting on fire. The young men were speaking with tongues, prophesying. What on earth did it mean? Only that Moody has been addressing them that afternoon! What manner of man is this? I cannot describe Moody's great meeting: I can only say that the people of Sunderland warmly supported the movement, in spite of their local spiritual advisers."

9. At the dawn of the 20th century, the Holy Spirit outpoured in abundance. It centered in the metropolis of Los Angeles and soon spread around the entire earth.

Lester Sumrall entered full-time service for God after experiencing what he recalls as the most dramatic and significant thing that ever happened to him.

At the age of 17 as he lay on a deathbed, suffering from tuberculosis, he received a vision: Suspended in midair to the right of his bed was a casket; on his left was a large open Bible. He heard these words: "Lester, which of these will you choose tonight?" He made his decision: He would preach the Gospel as long as he lived. When he awoke the next morning, he was completely healed.

In nearly 50 years of worldwide missionary evangelism, Dr. Sumrall has ministered in more than 100 countries, including Soviet Siberia, Russia, Tibet, and China.

Today, his evangelistic association, headquartered in South Bend, Indiana, is actively spreading God's Word. Dr. Sumrall's goal is to win 1,000,000 souls for the Kingdom of God. His ministry includes the World Harvest Bible College, radio and television stations, a teaching tape ministry, and numerous publications.

In addition to this, Dr. Sumrall is still deeply involved with ministry overseas.

For information regarding Lester Sumrall's monthly magazine, *World Harvest,* you may write:

Lester Sumrall
P. O. Box 12
South Bend, IN 46624